To
Joe & Helen
from Randy & Phyllis

Christmas 2012

The Stark bedroom and the
second floor landing arrayed
in holiday splendor.

Christmas

AT THE MANSION

AT THE MANSION
ITS MEMORIES AND MENUS

BY
JEAN CARNAHAN

Published by MMPI, L.L.C.
1999

To the Mansion "team"—
Paula Earls, Jerry Walsh, Norma Jean Davidson,
docents, security and maintenance personnel, Mary Pat Abele,
and the Missouri Mansion Preservation staff whose devotion to
the hospitality and traditions of the Mansion inspired this book.
Thanks for the Memories!

Designer	Jean Carnahan
Assistant Design and Layout	Scott Rule
	Mary Pat Abele
Architectural, Interior, and Food Photography	
	Alise O'Brien
Historical Document Photographer	Roger Berg
Table Setting Designs	Chris Carr
	Cindy Singer
Research	Jean Carnahan
	Chris Carr
Recipe Testing	Chef Jerry Walsh
	Norma Jean Davidson

Published 1999 by MMPI, L.L.C., a subsidiary of Missouri Mansion Preservation, Inc., Post Office Box 1133, Jefferson City, Missouri 65102.

ISBN 0-9668992-1-0
Printed and bound in the USA
by
Walsworth Publishing Company

CONTENTS

MEMORIES OF CHRISTMAS
1

MANTEL MAGIC
19

VICTORIAN TREES AND TRIMMINGS
29

HOLIDAY TABLES
43

FESTIVE MENUS

CHRISTMAS GALA 52
STATE DINNER 62 ❊ LEGISLATIVE DINNER 72
DOCENTS' LUNCHEON 80 ❊ SECRETARIES' LUNCHEON 86
AFTERNOON TEA 92 ❊ HOLIDAY BUFFET 108
FAMILY HOLIDAY DINNER 118
WINTER EVENINGS AT HOME 130

The Missouri State Christmas Tree features the official symbols of the Show-Me State. Created for the Governor's Mansion in 1999, the ornaments portray the state flower, the hawthorn; tree, the dogwood; bird, the bluebird; fish, the catfish; insect, the bumble bee; musical instrument, the fiddle; song, the *Missouri Waltz*; the Great Seal; and the flag of the state.

PREFACE

How sad it is to tear down the showy mantel displays . . . to remove the thousands of handmade ornaments from the trees . . . to discard the fading poinsettias.

I thought: if only I could sprinkle the Mansion with stardust and "poof" it would stay clothed forever in unfaded glory. That being impossible, I did the next best thing. I took pictures and recorded memories.

With the help of several skilled photographers, many of the holiday scenes of recent years have been preserved. The pictures were so spectacular that some were chosen for inclusion in the 1999 winter edition of *Victorian Homes and Lifestyles*.

Later when I saw copies of *A White House Christmas* and *Christmas Decorations from Williamsburg*, I was impressed with how favorably our decorations compared to those of other historic homes.

Thus inspired, I launched what turned into a nine-month project, writing and designing *Christmas at the Mansion: Its Memories and Menus*. Had I the foresight to leave off the recipe section, this book would have been far quicker to assemble. But realizing how often guests ask for our recipes, I decided it was worth the extra effort to include some Mansion menus.

I fretted over which ones to include since we serve food at such a variety of events, ranging from a formal Christmas Gala to casual lawn parties. Each year there are gatherings for children with disabilities, for arts award recipients, and for older workers. There are also commemorative observances of Martin Luther King, Jr.'s birthday, the Holocaust, and women's suffrage. There are teas for visiting ambassadors, Girl Scout troops, and relatives of former first families, as well as lunches for secretaries, lawmakers, and foreign delegations.

I resolved my problem by including nine menus spanning the range of entertaining at the Mansion. I included our most repeated recipes with an emphasis on holiday fare. Some are old, some new. Some fancy, some everyday. Some easy and others more difficult.

It was great fun testing each selection in the Mansion kitchen alongside our talented and good-natured chef, Jerry Walsh. Most of the recipes have been enjoyed by guests at one time or another, but serving amounts had to be adjusted for home cooking. I was fortunate, too, for the baking expertise of Norma Jean Davidson who tested the breads and cookies in her home kitchen in smaller batches than we normally cook at the Mansion.

I also leaned upon several other great cooks, Mel's sister-in-law, Oma Carnahan, and longtime friends and culinary wizards Nancy Mengel and Ethel Burton. I include my mother in that list of superb cooks also. Because she was a Virginian by heritage and food preference, our holiday meals always included country ham, spoon bread, cooked greens, and sweet potatoes. But the holiday meals of my childhood now conflict with the trendy cuisine of the nineties, forcing me to drop a favorite recipe too heavily laced with chocolate, sour cream, or real mayonnaise. I tried to convince myself that life was the better for it.

The task of capturing a Mansion Christmas on film was accomplished by architectural photographer Alise O'Brien of St. Louis. She took most of the interior and exterior views of the house, both for this book and my earlier work, *If Walls Could Talk*. Infinitely patient and artistic, she adapted well to food photography and graciously endured my input. A number of existing photographs were tracked down with the assistance of Jim Goodrich, director of The State Historical Society of Missouri, and State Archivist Ken Winn.

I am grateful also to Chris Carr and Cindy Singer for their expertise in holiday design and decorating, and to Bob Fennewald and Mary Jo Hilker who volunteer a week of their time each year to prepare the Mansion for Christmas.

In addition, Chris and Mary Pat Abele, executive director of Missouri Mansion Preservation, attended to the many details necessary in researching and publishing this book. When I look at similar volumes and see a listing of thirty or more staff members involved in a book project, I realize what "miracles" we perform with a small but dedicated team.

This portrayal of *Christmas at the Mansion: Its Memories and Menus* made 1999 a year-long celebration for all of us. During that time I often thought of Henry Van Dyke's poem about "Keeping Christmas" (see pages 140-141). He posed the thought—if we can keep Christmas for one day, why not forever? I agree.

Merry Christmas always!

Jean Carnahan
Jefferson City, Missouri
1999

A 19th-century Christmas card outlined with silk fringe expresses the sentiments of the holiday season.

It is good to be children sometimes,
And never better than at Christmas.
                           ~Charles Dickens

MEMORIES
OF CHRISTMAS

"Awaiting Santa's Arrival"—a scene from the
second floor landing of the living quarters.

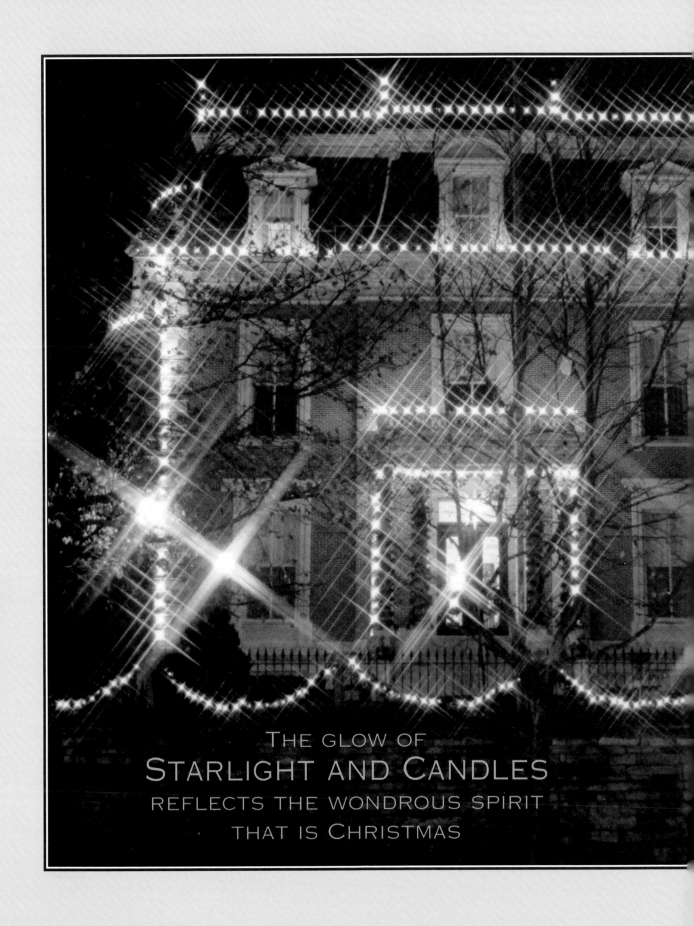

THE GLOW OF
STARLIGHT AND CANDLES
REFLECTS THE WONDROUS SPIRIT
THAT IS CHRISTMAS

U pon seeing the Mansion for the first time, eight-year-old Carey Shannon was thrilled by its grandeur. She called her new home "a real fairyland." She spoke of "huge rooms, magnificent furniture, magic carpets, and chandeliers ablaze with rainbows gleaming through crystal pendants."

That was 125 years ago. But even now, children—and adults as well—express much the same feeling, particularly at Christmas.

Today, the holiday season officially begins when the Governor and First Lady flip the switch that turns on the lights outlining the house and the giant tree on the Mansion lawn. An audible gasp can be heard among the thousands of visitors awaiting the magic moment.

Guests are in for more delights as they pass through the Mansion doorway, into an era of Victorian splendor. Crystal

At Christmas the Victorians opened their homes in a warm display of hospitality and Yuletide celebration as shown in this 19th-century lithograph.

Youngsters from poor families and children of prisoners were often entertained at boisterous Christmas parties at the Mansion.

chandeliers hang from gilded ceilings. Wide doorways open into rooms furnished with silk-upholstered chairs and ornately dressed windows.

From this colorful backdrop, the First Family greets several thousand holiday visitors during the two evenings set aside for the Christmas Candlelight Tours. For some it is their first trip to the Mansion; for others it is an annual family pilgrimage.

Over the last twenty-five years, Missouri's first families have marked the beginning of the holiday season in the Capital City with an open house.

Earlier residents of the executive home centered their holiday celebration primarily upon children. Youngsters from poor

families and the children of prisoners were often entertained at a boisterous Christmas party.

One year, Mrs. Jane Francis (1889-1893) held the children's party in the ballroom. Those attending were treated to a marionette show, as well as toys and fruits distributed by Santa Claus.

Without the aid of Santa, Governors Marmaduke, Folk, and Stephens each crawled beneath the sweeping branches of the Mansion Christmas tree to distribute oranges, dolls, and false faces to their young guests.

It is not known whether First Lady Lula Stone (1893-1897) continued the practice. But her husband, Governor William Stone, did invite

JUST BEFORE CHRISTMAS

by Eugene Field

The Missouri poet Eugene Field was a frequent visitor to the Governor's Mansion
during the term of Governor John Phelps (1877-1881).

Father calls me William, sister calls me Will,
Mother calls me Willie, but the fellers call me Bill!
Mighty glad I ain't a girl—ruther be a boy.
Without them sashes, curls, an' things that's worn by Fauntleroy!
Love to chawnk green apples an' go swimmin' in the lake—
Hate to take the castor-ile they give for belly-ache!
'Most all the time, the whole year round, there ain't no flies on me,
But jest 'fore Christmas I'm as good as I kin be!

Got a yeller dog named Sport, sick him on the cat;
First thing she knows she doesn't know where she is at!
Got a clipper sled, an' when us kids goes out to slide,
'Long comes the grocery cart, an' we all hook a ride!
But sometimes when the grocery man is worried an' cross,
He reaches at us with his whip, an' larrups up his hoss,
An' then I laff an' holler, "Oh, ye never teched me!"
But jest 'fore Christmas I'm as good as I kin be!

Gran'ma says she hopes that when I git to be a man,
I'll be a missionarer like her oldest brother, Dan,
As we et up by the cannibals that lives in Ceylon's Isle,
Where every prospeck pleases, an' only man is vile!
But gran'ma she has never been to see a Wild West show,
Nor read the Life of Daniel Boone, or else I guess she'd know
That Buff'lo Bill an' cow-boys is good enough for me!
Except' jest 'fore Christmas, when I'm good as I kin be!

And then old Sport he hangs around, so solemn-like an' still,
His eyes they seem a'sayin': "What's the matter, little Bill?"
The old cat sneaks down off her perch an' wonders what's become
Of them two enemies of hern that used to make things hum!
But I am so perlite an' 'tend so earnestly to biz,
That mother says to father: "How improved our Willie is!"
But father, havin' been a boy hisself, suspicions me
When, jest 'fore Christmas, I'm as good as I kin be!

For Christmas, with its lots an' lots of candies,
    cake, an' toys,
Was made, they say, for proper kids,
    an' not for naughty boys;
So wash yer face an' bresh yer hair,
    an' mind year p's and q's
An' don't bust out yer pantaloons,
    and don't wear out yer shoes;
Say "Yessum" to the ladies,
    an' "Yessur" to the men,
An' when they's company, don't pass
    yer plate for pie again;
But, thinkin' of the things yer'd like
    to see upon that tree,
Jest 'fore Christmas be as good as yer
    kin be!

Missouri poet Eugene Field as portrayed
on the wall of the Governor's office in
the State Capitol.

A snowball fight on the front lawn was a hearty and enjoyable pastime for Victorian families.

friends to share his famous eggnog blend, featuring the best whisky from his native state of Kentucky.

Not every Christmas at the Mansion was a happy celebration for its residents. Each of the deaths in the first families occurred during the holiday season. The first was in 1882 with the loss of Governor and Mrs. T. T. Crittenden's nine-year-old daughter. Carrie Crittenden, "The yellow-haired pet of the family," died of diphtheria just five days before Christmas.

Governor John Marmaduke succumbed to pneumonia several days after Christmas 1887, on the date set for the children's party.

First Lady Mary Dockery died on New Year's Day 1903 and her funeral was held that evening in place of the traditional Military Ball previously scheduled.

Despite these holiday tragedies and the occasional interruption caused by war and depressions, Christmas was generally a happy time at the Mansion.

Each first family tried to maintain their holiday traditions.

Governor and Mrs. Herbert Hadley (1909-1913) encouraged their three children to put kernels of corn on the window ledge for Santa's reindeer, just as they always did at home.

Mrs. Guy Park (1933-1937) added a

A 1930s CHRISTMAS

The earliest record of a lighted Christmas display on the Mansion lawn was during the administration of Governor Guy Park and First Lady Eleanora Park (1933-1937).

Even the Great Depression could not dampen the spirit of Christmas at the Mansion. First Lady Eleanora Park puts the finishing touches on the tree in the Great Hall during the 1930s.

A 1940s CHRISTMAS

During the bleak days of World War II, Governor Forrest Donnell (1941-1945) and his family pause to read the Christmas story in their Webster Groves home.

9

festive touch to the house and lawn with the addition of Christmas lights, but the Forrest Donnell family (1941-1945) were forced to more austerity. Living in the Mansion during World War II, the family endured the shortages and subdued celebration along with the rest of the state and nation.

Nonetheless, the Donnells tried to make the season one of happy remembrances. Returning to their Webster Groves home during the holdays, the family gathered in the living room for a responsive reading of the Christmas story just as they had done throughout their lives.

During the postwar era, the Forrest Smith family (1949-1953) returned the lights to the Mansion lawn. Mrs. Smith also found the long bannister of the Grand Stairway a perfect showcase for the many greeting cards she received.

Years later Mrs. Christopher "Kit" Bond (1973-1977 and 1981-1985) initiated the Christmas Candlelight Tours during her time as First Lady. In addition to the charm the candles provided, the dim lighting was a reminder of the energy crisis and the need for Missourians to conserve electricity.

Mrs. Joseph Teasdale (1977-1981) included disabled children in musical performances and invited sheltered workshop employees to make ornaments for the Mansion tree.

The family's three young sons no doubt enjoyed a gift to the Mansion from the American Association of Railroaders—an electric train. Each year members of the group return to view and repair the train that is traditionally on display during the holidays.

The Mel Carnahan family (1993-Present) provides a festive atmosphere for the community with their enhancement of the Candlelight Tours. At Christmas the Mansion is outlined in lights and a thirty-to-forty-foot evergreen is installed on the lawn. Baby camels and reindeer, as well as Santa Claus, greet visitors attending the traditional open house. The First Family hosts Christmas teas and a Victorian-style dinner party during December to help raise funds for Mansion preservation and restoration projects.

As the 20th century draws to a close, the stately old home remains a symbol of Missouri's heritage. It has housed fifty of her governors and borne witness to tragedy and triumph during its 128 years. Clad in an elegance of yesteryear, the stately Mansion still retains its hold on all those who live or visit within its walls.

A 1950s Christmas

(Left) President Harry Truman gets in the spirit of the season delivering holiday gifts from his house in Independence, Missouri; (right) First Lady Mildred Smith strings her holiday cards from the chandelier and bannister; (below) an outdoor lighting display during the Smith administration.

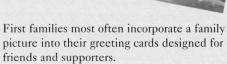

First families most often incorporate a family picture into their greeting cards designed for friends and supporters.

(Clockwise from top left): Christopher "Kit" Bond family; Mel Carnahan family's 1998 card and 1993 card, "First Christmas in the Mansion;" Joseph Teasdale family; and Donnelly family Christmas greeting.

Governor and Mrs. Phil M. Donnelly
extend Greetings and
Best Wishes for
Christmas and the New Year

Christmas Cards

(Clockwise from top left): Winter scene from the card of the John Dalton family; Forrest Smith family; John Ashcroft family; Mel Carnahan family; Warren Hearnes family.

SCENES
OF THE
SEASON

THE TREES ARRIVE. . .

(Top and lower left) The Christmas trees arrive at the Mansion during the week after Thanksgiving. (Lower right) Cindy Singer decorates the Mansion Christmas tree with the thousands of ornaments submitted by school children.

THE MUSIC SOUNDS. . .

(Top) Cindy, Ashley, and Randy Singer, dressed in Victorian garb, are among the many carolers at the Mansion each year. (Lower left) Madrigal players perform traditional tunes upon old instruments during the Christmas Gala. (Lower right) Docent Jimmy Kay Sanders strums the Mansion harp.

(Above) Two former first ladies appear to be looking over the children's coats piled high on a parlor settee as First Lady Jean Carnahan (right) reads a Christmas story to her young visitors.

THE CHILDREN GATHER . . .

Youngsters perform from the steps of the Grand Stairway during the annual Candlelight Tours.

Six-month-old Nathan Weil has his first visit with Santa during a tour of the Mansion.

(Above left) Andrew Carnahan, five-year-old grandson of Governor and Mrs. Mel Carnahan; (upper right) a Nativity scene featured at the Mansion; (lower right) the Herman family lights the Hanukkah candelabra—a gift to the Mansion that came from Jerusalem.

Can I forget those stockings,
Filled from top to bulging toe
By mother's hand at Christmas-time
Within the long ago?
~"My Christmas Day" by Helen D'Aubry Durana

MANTEL MAGIC

(Facing page) The Great Hall fireplace, Christmas 1998.

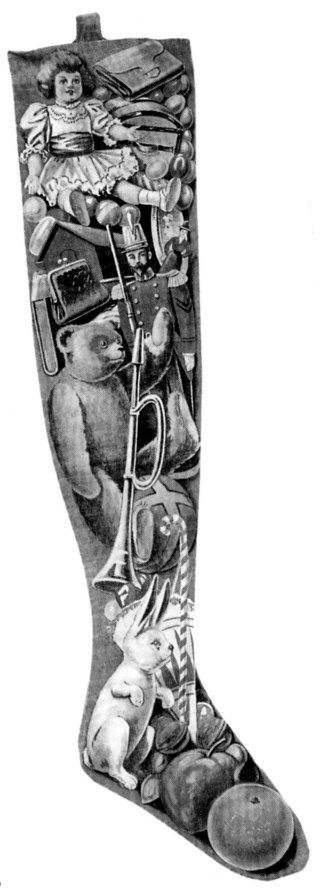

The six children of Governor and Mrs. B. Gratz Brown waited impatiently for the arrival of Santa at the Mansion in 1872. They had moved into the new Mansion eleven months earlier, thus creating the longest possible wait for the next Christmas.

Surely, Santa would have no trouble finding them. The spacious, three-story house with the nine fireplaces was the finest in town. Still, like other homes of the day, it was cold and drafty with no central heating or indoor bathrooms.

Though the Victorian home lacked many of our modern conveniences, there was more than enough space for an evergreen tree in the parlor with the seventeen-foot ceiling.

As yet, however, there were no electric lights to brighten the tree; no brightly colored wrappings for the packages beneath it. Nor was there a phonograph to fill the house with tunes of the season or an electric train to run along the parquet floor.

(Left) A 24-inch linen stocking painted with pictures of toys popular in Victorian times. (Top right) A Thomas Nast drawing appearing in *Harper's Weekly* in 1872, the first year that Christmas was celebrated at the new Mansion.

A Victorian "Night before Christmas" is reenacted by six-year-old Merritt Gibbs in the Crittenden bedroom of the Mansion.

But there were nine fireplaces from which the children could hang their Christmas stockings. Most choose the mantel in the Great Hall, the largest one nearest the door.

At one time all the mantels were made of Italian marble. But in 1905, an out-of-control blaze destroyed the fireplace in the Great Hall and spread to the dining room and upper floor before being extinguished.

The replacement mantel fashioned from walnut and emblazoned with the state seal now dominates the entry. Children still hang their stockings from the restored mantel, but there are no wood burning fireplaces in the house. Today gas logs bring a warm glow to the brightly decorated rooms and a reassurance to Mansion hostesses.

The stately marble fireplaces have also been the back drop for the weddings of Henrietta Park Krause (1933), Jim Tom Blair (1958), and Lynn Hearnes (1970)–the only

(Upper left) Mrs. Forrest Smith displays the decorations in the Great Hall during the early 1950s; (upper right) a hand stitched fireplace screen decorates the parlor hearth; (bottom left) a more ornate rendition of the same mantel during the second administration of Governor Christopher "Kit" Bond in the 1980s.

offspring of first families to be married in the house.

The library fireplace features a handsome walnut carved clock and epergne set—the purchase of Governor John Marmaduke (1885-1887) during his travels in Europe. The set arrived after his death and was given to the Mansion in his memory.

In recent years, mantels have become a showcase for elaborate Christmas trimmings. During the 1950s, Mrs. Smith bedecked the mantels with small lighted trees and candles. Years later, the Bond family delighted their young son with a display of drums and teddy bears nestled in the mantel greenery. Colorful, handstitched stockings were hung by the chimney and a tray of milk and cookies put out for Santa's visit.

Today the Victorian mantels continue to be a dramatic backdrop for baubles and bows, a warm reflection of an old-fashioned Christmas.

(Upper left) The second-floor Stark bedroom mantel decorated with poinsettias and Meissen candelabras. (Upper right) The Christmas 1996 parlor fireplace; (bottom right) brightly colored lemons complement the library's yellow and green motif.

The Christmas Stocking

The stockings were hung by the chimney with care,
In hopes that St. Nicholas that soon would be there.

The old poem, "'Twas the Night Before Christmas," proclaims the custom of hanging a stocking from the fireplace mantel. But securing a stocking to the marble mantels of the Mansion was something of a problem. The task was made a lot easier after the mantel in the Great Hall was replaced with walnut in 1905 following a destructive fire.

The holiday practice of filling stockings with goodies came from a European tradition. According to legend, three spinster sisters hung their stockings by the hearth to dry on Christmas Eve.

Too poor for a dowry, they hoped for a miracle that would enable them to marry. St. Nicholas, knowing their plight, dropped three bags of gold coins down the chimney into each stocking.

Victorian children found not only coins, but small toys, fruits, and candies stuffed into their Christmas stockings. The fear that Santa might leave no more than a lump of coal in the stocking of naughty youngsters went a long way toward improving their behavior during the weeks before Christmas. (See Eugene Field's poem, "Just Before Christmas," pages 6-7.)

In today's homes, ornately stitched stockings are often personalized with the names of each family member. But the old-fashioned custom of searching the stockings for small gifts is often ignored by children who are more attracted to the larger presents left by Santa under the glitzy Christmas tree.

(Facing page) The Great Hall fireplace complemented by dried flowers, pinecones, and poinsettias.

(Upper left) The parlor mantel is draped with a fringed scarf and highlighted with candles.
(Upper right) The walnut mantel of the Great Hall appears to be in bloom with flowers.
(Bottom) One of the two dining room fireplace mantels; (facing page) the library decorated in
the theme "Angels We Have Heard on High" features a Lyon and Healy harp, a gift from the
Joyce Pillsbury family and Mary and Don Wainwright.

The holly's up, the house is all bright,
The tree is ready, the candles alight;
Rejoice and be glad, all children tonight!

~From a 19th century German carol

VICTORIAN
TREES & TRIMMINGS

(Facing page) The 22-foot Christmas tree filling the Nook beneath the
Grand Stairway holds more than one thousand handmade ornaments created
by Missouri school children. (Above) One of more than 400 scherenschnitte
ornaments—"scissors' cuttings" in German—from the Smithsonian
Institution's exhibit that decorated the Mansion tree in 1989.

Now Christmas is come, let's beat up the drum
And call our neighbors together.
~Washington Irving

amiliar scents and sounds fill the air and traditional holiday tunes drift through the staid Victorian parlors.

It is Christmas at the Mansion.

Decorating begins early with the arrival of the Mansion "elves." Wearing red, pointed caps and colorful aprons, these floral designers are about to transform the old house into a merry wonderland.

In preparation, workmen hoist several trees into place, releasing a woodland fragrance throughout the house. The oversized evergreens have been rescued from construction sites for their final moments of glory. The largest occupies the front lawn. Several others—white pine and spruce—find spacious surroundings in the seventeen-foot-tall rooms.

Ladders, metal tables, and boxes of decorations temporarily replace silk settees and nineteenth-century furnishings.

Work begins first on the main tree. Its sweeping, lower branches fill the Nook and the top limbs push upward through the opening of the spiraling stairway.

With the aid of scaffolding, and a pole and hook, the trimming begins. The tree comes alive with the addition of ornaments—gingerbread men, sleds, snowmen, rocking horses, dreidels,

(Facing page) The third floor Squires' Room decorated in a Moorish style typical of a 19th-century drawing room.
(Above) A sideboard display of old musical instruments.

The Mansion lawn lighted for the Christmas season.

snowflakes, and tussie-mussies—all handmade by school children. Beneath the tree, antique bears, dolls, and soldiers wait to delight both young and old.

The creative elves also cast their magic upon the smaller trees. Gold mesh bows snuggle between sand dollars and crocheted snowflakes. Angels, harps, and trumpets are tucked into the pine branches.

More boughs and baubles brighten the granite porch columns, as well as the crystal-prismed chandeliers.

The great silver punch bowl, which once served aboard the battleship USS *Missouri*, is polished to a high luster and festooned with bright, silk flowers.

By the end of the week, all is in place for the annual Candlelight Tours.

Decorators, weary from long days and nights, step back to admire their handiwork. Smiles of satisfaction abound. Workers share a

The silver punch bowl from the battleship USS *Missouri* features the Great Seal of the state. On special occasions, the 113-pint bowl above features a stunning display of fresh flowers.

pizza from a cardboard carton that is spread atop a work table strewn with ribbon fragments, spare ornaments, and glue guns.

The final touch comes when over two hundred poinsettias arrive. The pink, red, white, and sometimes yellow-blossomed plants are banked beside the hearths and columns.

Custodians wielding push brooms and vacuums remove pine needles and glitter before the floors get their final buffing.

Symbols of the sacred season—the Hanukkah candelabra and nativity scene—are placed in quiet corners, waiting to be discovered.

As the lights are dimmed, the old rooms appear to drift back in time as the soft glow of candles and fireplaces cast their warmth upon the house.

In a few hours, the doors will swing open to holiday visitors.

Dressed in Victorian finery, the stately old Mansion, like a grand dame of yesteryear, will once again enchant her guests with the joys and glories of Christmas.

(Facing page) The parlor features a tall slender tree topped with peacock feathers.

O' Christmas Tree

Nothing does more to rekindle warm memories than a brightly decorated Christmas tree.

Today's trees evolved from early Victorian models that came into vogue in the United States in the 1850s and 1860s. When Queen Victoria's family decorated a small table top tree with fruits, nuts, berries, and cookies, Americans couldn't resist the idea.

Children were especially delighted by the edible ornaments that could be pulled from the branches and eaten on Christmas morning.

By the 1870s, much taller trees were being dragged into American homes—the bigger the tree the more affluent the family. At the Governor's Mansion, the Great Hall with its seventeen-foot ceiling, provided the perfect location for an oversized tree.

Families of this era decorated the tree branches with small gifts, flags, and ribbons.

A dyed goose feather tree.

With the appearance of glass ornaments in the 1880s, trees took on an even more festive look. However, the addition of small candles required caution and buckets of water were kept close by to douse any flames that got out of hand.

The Capital City with its largely German population no doubt followed the European custom of creating a putz beneath the holiday tree—a little village or nativity scene enclosed with a fence.

Also popular was the dyed goose feather tree. While not as handsome as a live evergreen, it could be left in place longer and used from year to year.

By the 1890s, imported ornaments made of puffy, white cotton batting came into vogue (see Santa on previous page). The animal and human shapes were enlivened with painted faces or paper masks. More interest was added to the tree with the use of "scraps"—the colorful, embossed paper designs clipped by women and children.

By the turn of the century, tinsel was added to tree branches, giving rise to arguments as to whether it should be applied in clumps or individual strands.

A crowning touch came with the introduction of the tree topper, featuring angels, stars, or spiraled glass ornaments.

Today the Mansion Christmas tree is brightened with lights and simple Victorian-style ornaments made by hundreds of Missouri school children. The tree stands most often in the Nook where there is ample space for a tall pine to soar upward through the open ceiling above the spiraling stairway.

Governor and Mrs. Carnahan closed out the century with the holiday theme "O' Christmas Tree"—a salute to the many versions of the decorated tree. Also new in 1999 was the Missouri Tree decorated with official symbols of the state's heritage—the bluebird, state seal, fiddle, dogwood, catfish, bumble bee, hawthorn, and music scrolls imprinted with the "Missouri Waltz."

Trees & Trimmings...

(Top border) The ornate grillwork that crowns
the mansard roof of the Mansion; (left) a tree
featuring white sand dollars; (upper right) a dining
room light fixture dressed for the holidays; (lower
right) a front porch display of pineapples—a
traditional symbol of hospitality.

A Touch of Wonder

(Top left) The library gasolier trimmed with lemons and greenery; (upper right) a dining room centerpiece in the living quarters; (bottom right) a front door wreath; (lower left) a 19th-century ceiling decorated for the holidays.

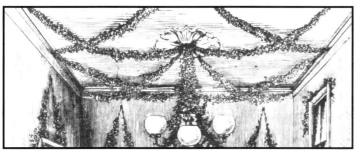

The double parlor banked with poinsettias.

CHRISTMAS DINNER

We enjoyed Governor Miller's old-fashioned and warm-hearted hospitality, and had a glorious time generally.

~ J. S. Rollins, following his visit in 1831 to the first Missouri Governor's Mansion.

HOLIDAY TABLES

(Facing page) The Mansion dining table awaits Christmas guests.

(Above) A 1980s holiday dinner set in the parlor looking towards the Grand Stairway; (below) the dining room in the second-floor living quarters. (Facing page) The first-floor dining room table set with the USS *Missouri* silverware, goblets, and candelabras.

The southern heritage of many of Missouri's first families was most apparent in the food served at the Mansion.

For years the beaten biscuit—long a staple of plantation life—was served at the Mansion both for holiday gatherings and everyday fare. The tasty biscuit was literally beaten into shape with a flat iron, or by using a beaten biscuit machine. Served with a slice of country ham, the ubiquitous biscuit appeared on Mansion menus until the 1950s.

A look at Mansion tables of yesteryears reminds us not only of our state's heritage, but also of our ever-changing tastes. The first large social event in the executive home featured a delicacy that would hardly be acceptable today—a pyramid of pitted snipe. Mrs. B. Gratz Brown (1871-1873) served the sparrow-sized birds to nearly two thousand guests who jammed the halls and stairways to view the new house.

Mrs. Henry Hardin (1875-1877) was more austere with her entertaining, preferring small dinner parties without music, dancing, or alcohol.

However, her successor was less inhibited. Governor Phelps' daughter initiated her time as Mansion hostess with a bountiful buffet spread over a fifty-foot table. Twenty decorated cakes lined the table along with varieties of ice creams molded into swans, doves, and dolphins.

"The table fairly groaned with platters of ham, turkey, buffalo tongue, oysters—fried, stewed, and on the half-shell—broiled quail,

chicken salad, and all kinds of game." However, she declined to serve rum—a favored and expected refreshment of the day—causing some guests to come prepared with their own beverage.

A subsequent Mansion hostess, Kate Morrow, said she had only one instruction from the widower Governor Alexander Dockery. He wanted to be served some form of chicken every day. "Needless to say, he got it," she recalled.

Poultry also showed up on the Mansion table when Mrs. Herbert Hadley (1909-1913) served as First Lady. One year she served six hundred chickens brought in from the family farm located on the outskirts of the Capital City.

The gracious First Lady, a Republican, had no qualms about extending the Mansion's hospitality to the three time presidential contender, William Jennings Bryan, a Democrat. He arrived late one evening, missing the fried chicken dinner Mrs. Hadley had prepared especially for him. The First Lady was crest fallen when she sat the meal out again and Bryan announced that he would just as soon have "a big bowl of milk and bread."

In addition to providing fresh produce for the Mansion table, the Hadley's farm provided a hunting ground for the Governor and his friends. One of Mrs. Hadley's wild game dinners included roast quail, possum, 'coon, wild turkey, squirrel stew, fried rabbit, venison, and wild duck—all shot on the outskirts of town.

But most often Mrs. Hadley served a standard sit-down meal. "We always had the same menu, and I helped in the pantry," she recalled. "We had soup, a big chicken pie at each end of the table, vegetables, beaten biscuits, a salad, ice cream, cake, and small coffees."

Planning meals to fit the occasion and the guests has always been a major concern of Mansion hostesses. In addition, Mrs. Henry Caulfield (1929-1933) fretted over the protocol and seating arrangements for the visit of the Japanese Ambassador.

Having resolved the situation with a call to the state department, she treated her foreign guests to a formal American meal. The unusual breakfast menu—a treat to the American palate, but not likely to the Japanese—consisted of grapefruit supreme,

A formal turn-of-the-century dining room table during the administration of Governor Lon Stephens and his wife, Maggie, one of the Mansion's most flamboyant hostesses.

chicken a la king on toast, fresh peas in carrot baskets, new potatoes with Hollandaise sauce, Parker House rolls, and strawberry ice cream and cake.

A later First Lady, Mrs. Jerry Dalton (1961-1965), earned a reputation as a gracious Southern hostess, serving such Bootheel favorites as amber pie, baked grits, and Ozark pudding. Her husband felt that "a days eating wasn't complete without hot biscuits or fresh cornbread." According to Jerry, the Governor was especially fond of country ham and green beans or cornfield peas seasoned with pork and simmered in an iron pot.

Governor and Mrs. Warren Hearnes (1965-1973) had the honor of entertaining their fellow governors and first ladies who

Guests enjoy a formal dinner party with Governor and Mrs. Herbert Hadley (1909-1913).

twice visited Missouri for a governors' conference. Dining at the Lake of the Ozarks, members of the Mid-Western Governors' Conference enjoyed a formal meal that included vichyssoise, beef Wellington, and strawberries Romanoff.

Mrs. Hearnes also wanted to serve a fine meal to Senator Edward "Ted" Kennedy when he showed up unexpectedly in Jefferson City. But it was the cook's day off. The indomitable First Lady found some ground beef in the kitchen and cooked king-size hamburgers for her New England visitor. When Mrs. Hearnes apologized for such simple fare, the gracious Senator replied that hamburger was one of his favorites.

With much more warning, Carolyn Bond unleashed her culinary expertise on Secretary of State and Mrs. Henry Kissinger. The couple breakfasted on French toast a la Reine, melon rings, orange juice, and sweet rolls before visiting the State Capitol.

Food preparation and service for large groups has always been a challenge to

First Lady Jerry Dalton (1961-1965) with a coffee table decorated for the holiday season.

Mansion hostesses and cooks. Early first ladies sought professional help when the situation demanded more elegant fare than could be provided locally. St. Louis caterers and floral designers were brought in for festive occasions.

In one instance, these imported cooks worked in the kitchen for a week getting ready for Silas Woodson's (1873-1875) inaugural reception. Apparently, First Lady Jennie Woodson delighted the capital community with an exquisite table described as "a marvel of confectionery art and floral decoration."

Such accomplishments were exceedingly difficult. Fine dinnerware was often in short supply at the Mansion. With little or no funding from budget-minded legislators, most first families had to make do on their own, even into the 20th century.

A well-to-do family provided their own fine serving pieces, but most residents were left with the missed-matched, hand-me-downs from previous administrations.

Even those few hostesses blessed with fine linen, silver, and catering service found entertaining a frustration. Moving food from the basement kitchen to the upper floors was done by dumbwaiter—an awkward arrangement that made it impossible to serve food at the correct temperature.

Goblet from the USS *Missouri* silver service.

Eventually, one First Lady refused to tolerate the slow, inefficient food service. Mrs. Lloyd Stark (1937-1941) began the task of major renovation. The hearty First Lady took one look at the dreary, rat-infested kitchen with the dirt floor and began one of the most extensive remodelings the house ever underwent. The addition of a kitchen wing on the first floor made modern food service possible for the first time.

Today the Mansion features a stainless steel, restaurant-class kitchen capable of serving more than one hundred guests for a sit-down meal and several hundred at a reception.

Current menus often reflect the state's ethnic and cultural diversity. Mrs. Bond delighted guests with Mexican courses, and Mrs. Carnahan entertained legislators with a variety of cuisines, including German, Irish, Asian, and African-American foods. Christmas gatherings today range from small afternoon teas with a Girl Scout troop to gala black-tie events with dancing, Madrigal singers, and strolling violinists.

Hospitality continues to be the hallmark of the Victorian home and a pleasure to all who dine within the Mansion walls.

HISTORY AND HOSPITALITY MEET AT THE MANSION TABLE
NOTABLE GUESTS AT THE MANSION

Left Column: Grand Duke Alexis of Russia, Joseph Pulitzer, William Jennings Bryan, Barbara Bush, Walter Cronkite. Middle Column: General George Custer, Jefferson Davis, President Harry Truman, Henry Kissinger. Right Column: King Kalakaua, Eugene Field, Senator Edward Kennedy, Prime Minister Edward Heath, Tipper Gore.

The dessert was splendid as ever,
With its golden oranges,
Brown nuts, and . . . apple jelly . . .
Christmas was as it had always been.

~George Eliot, "The Mill on the Floss"

FESTIVE MENUS

(Facing page) The dining room bedecked with a massive
arrangement of dried roses. (Above) Zoë Bednar samples
a Mansion gingerbread.

Christmas Gala

MAPLE GLAZED SCALLOPS

12 garlic cloves, large, cut lengthwise
 4 tablespoons butter (½ stick), divided
18 scallops, large
    salt and pepper
 ¼ cup maple syrup
 ¼ cup apple cider
 ¼ cup dry Champagne
 3 tablespoons shallots, chopped
 3 tablespoons fresh chives, chopped, divided

Bring garlic to boil in small saucepan of water; drain. Repeat process and set aside. Melt 2 tablespoons butter in heavy skillet over high heat. Season scallops with salt and pepper. Add to skillet and sauté until cooked through, about 3 minutes per side.

Transfer scallops to platter. Cover with foil to keep warm. Without cleaning skillet, add garlic, syrup, and cider. Boil until liquid is reduced to a glaze, about 3 minutes.

Add Champagne, shallots, and 2 tablespoons chives to skillet. Boil until liquid is reduced to sauce consistency, about 4 minutes. Add remaining 2 tablespoons butter. Whisk until melted. Season with salt and pepper. Pour sauce over scallops; sprinkle with remaining 1 tablespoon of chives.

Serves 4-6

Menu Selections from
Christmas Galas, 1993-1998

Maple Glazed Scallops

Mixed Greens, Pears,
and Gorgonzola
with Basil Vinaigrette

Beef Medallion with
Brandy Cream Sauce

Asparagus with Orange Butter

Crab-Stuffed Prawns

Garlic Potato Mounds

Mansion Dinner Rolls

Pumpkin Cheesecake

(Facing page) The Masion lawn blanketed with snow. The residence was painted white during the late 1930s. Thirty years later, the home was returned to its natural pink brick finish.

MIXED GREENS, PEARS, AND
GORGONZOLA WITH BASIL VINAIGRETTE

This Basil Viniagrette is the Mansion's most requested recipe. Keep it on hand for any green salad.

¾ pound mixed salad greens
3   Bosc pears, halved, cored, and thinly sliced
      lengthwise
½ cup dried cranberries (optional)
⅔ cup pecans, toasted and chopped
½ pound Gorgonzola cheese, crumbled

Combine mixed greens, pears, dried cranberries, and pecans in large bowl.

Lightly dress salad just before serving. Refrigerate unused portion of vinaigrette. Crumble cheese over top of salad.

BASIL VINAIGRETTE

2-3 garlic cloves, chopped
  ½ cup sugar
  ¾ cup fresh basil, chopped
  ½ teaspoon salt
  ½ teaspoon black pepper
  ½ cup cider vinegar
  1   cup salad oil

Using a food processor, blend garlic, sugar, basil, salt, and pepper until basil is chopped very fine. Add vinegar and blend. Pour in oil slowly and blend until smooth.

Serves 12

Mixed Greens, Pears, and Gorgonzola

BEEF MEDALLION
WITH BRANDY CREAM SAUCE

A stunning entree for a special dinner party.

2 tablespoons butter (¼ stick), divided
1 tablespoon shallots, chopped
3 garlic cloves, large, chopped
2 tablespoons fresh parsley, chopped, divided
1 teaspoon brown sugar
⅔ cup canned beef broth
2 tablespoons brandy
¼ teaspoon course ground pepper
¼ cup light cream
   salt and pepper
4 beef tenderloin steaks, 4-5 ounces each, about 1-inch thick

Melt 1 tablespoon butter in skillet over medium heat. Add shallots, garlic, 1 tablespoon parsley and sauté over medium heat until tender, about 4 minutes. Add brown sugar, stir 1 minute. Add broth, brandy, and pepper, simmering until sauce is reduced, about 6 minutes. Add cream.

Sprinkle steaks with salt and pepper. Melt remaining 1 tablespoon butter in large skillet over medium-high heat. Add steaks and cook to desired doneness, about 5 minutes per side for medium-rare.

Transfer steaks to plates. Spoon sauce over steaks. Sprinkle with remaining 1 tablespoon parsley.

Serves 4

Beef Medallion with Brandy Cream Sauce, Crab-Stuffed Prawns,
Asparagus with Orange Butter, and Garlic Potato Mounds

ASPARAGUS WITH ORANGE BUTTER

1 pound asparagus
1 orange, halved
1 tablespoon Grand Marnier

1 tablespoon white wine vinegar
8 tablespoons (1 stick) cold unsalted butter

Trim and peel asparagus. Steam until tender, about 4 to 5 minutes. Squeeze orange and strain juice.
Reserve both pulp and juice. In a saucepan, combine orange juice, Grand Marnier, and vinegar.
Cook over medium heat until sauce is reduced to 2 tablespoons.

Remove from heat and whisk butter into liquid, one tablespoon at a time, until thick and creamy.
Do not reheat or butter will melt. If mixture becomes too thick, or butter refuses to soften, hold pan
over simmering water to warm slightly.

Stir in orange pulp and spoon butter over hot asparagus.

Serves 4

CRAB-STUFFED PRAWNS

May be prepared a day ahead and refrigerated until ready to cook.

8 large prawns, peeled and deveined with tail intact
8 tablespoons (1 stick) butter, melted, divided
3 green onions, chopped fine
2 tablespoons carrot, chopped fine
2 tablespoons green pepper, chopped fine
2 tablespoons celery, chopped fine
1 teaspoon garlic, minced
2 (6-ounce) cans lump crabmeat or fresh crabmeat
1 teaspoon Dijon mustard
2 tablespoons Parmesan cheese, grated
¾ cup bread crumbs
1 egg, lightly beaten
  salt and pepper
¼ cup white wine

Butterfly prawns starting at underside and cutting toward tail; fan open. Place cut side on greased cookie sheet. Sauté vegetables and garlic in 4 tablespoons butter. Drain crab and place into pan; sauté until tender. Combine crab, vegetable mixture, mustard, cheese, bread crumbs, and egg in medium bowl. Season with salt and pepper to taste.

Roll stuffing into balls and place one atop each prawn, pushing down gently until prawn is covered. Fan tail over top of stuffing.

Melt remaining 4 tablespoons butter, combine with wine, and drizzle over prawns. Cook at 350 degrees for 12 to 15 minutes or until done.

Serves 4

The first Mansion Gala was held on January 24, 1872, three days after Governor B. Gratz Brown and his family moved into the new three-story hilltop Mansion.

In 1996, a costumed reenactment of the occasion was held at the Mansion. Guests wore Victorian clothing and danced to the tunes of the time.

The menu, however, was quite different from the 1872 event when the featured table attraction was a pyramid of spitted snipe.

GARLIC POTATO MOUNDS

1   whole head of garlic (about 6 cloves)
    dash of olive oil
1 ½ pounds Yukon potatoes, peeled, and cut in pieces
½   cup light cream
¼   cup low-fat sour cream
4   tablespoons (½ stick) butter
3   tablespoons chives, chopped
    salt and white pepper to taste

Cut off top of garlic bulb; drizzle the garlic with olive oil. Wrap in aluminum foil and bake at 300 degrees for 30 minutes. Squeeze garlic from cloves and mash with fork.

Boil potatoes until soft; drain. Purée garlic and cream in food processor until smooth. Mash potatoes along with garlic cream, sour cream, and butter. Add chives, salt, and white pepper to taste. Mound each potato serving on plate and insert a potato frame, if desired.

Serves 4

A favorite family dish dressed up for company.

POTATO FRAMES

1   long Idaho russet potato
    vegetable oil spray
    parsley leaves

Slice potato very thinly lengthwise using a mandolin or food slicer. Spray cooking sheet with vegetable oil and place 1 potato slice on sheet for each frame needed. Place flat leaf parsley on top. Top with a second thin slice, continuing with other sets for as many as are needed. Spray each set with oil.

Cover cookie sheet with another cookie sheet and place a skillet on top to weight down firmly. Place in oven at 350 degrees for 15 to 20 minutes or until frames become crisp and parsley is firmly encased in frames. To serve, stand frame upright in mashed potato mound.

This is a showy presentation for any dinner plate.

MANSION DINNER ROLLS

For a party, cut dough into smaller size rolls. Bake rolls, slice, and insert thin pieces of country ham. If desired, spread ham-rolls with a small amount of mayonnaise mixed with a bit of mustard and prepared horseradish.

2 packages yeast
½ cup plus 2 tablespoons sugar, divided
1 cup plus 2 tablespoons warm water (rolls rise best if water is 110-115 degrees)
⅓ cup unsalted butter, melted
1 teaspoon salt
3 eggs
5 cups flour, divided

Dissolve yeast and 2 tablespoons sugar in water. Let yeast activate. Add remaining sugar, butter, salt, and eggs; mix until eggs are well beaten. Add 2 cups flour, mixing well. Stir in another 3 cups of flour.

Turn out on lightly floured board and knead one minute. Place dough in greased bowl. Cover and let rise in warm place for 2 hours. Punch down; let rise again until double. Roll out dough and cut in desired size. Let rolls rise in pan for 30 minutes. Bake at 375 degrees for 10 to 15 minutes. May be frozen after baking, thawed, and rewarmed.

Makes 4 dozen small rolls

1997 Holiday Gala
December 12, 1997

Scallops with Glazed Garlic and Champagne Sauce
Mixed Greens, Pear, and Roquefort Salad
Dressed in a Balsamic Vinaigrette
Grilled Rack of Lamb and
Spinach Artichoke Stuffed Chicken
with Basil Cream Sauce
Potatoes with Caramelized Onions
Asparagus Bundles with Hollandaise Sauce
Mansion Sourdough Rolls
Dessert Buffet
Fruit, Coconut Meringue, and Lemon Meringue Tartletts
Croquembouche
Assorted Cheesecakes - Amaretto Peach, Chocolate Turtle,
White Chocolate Raspberry, and Chocolate Covered Strawberry
Decadent Chocolate Delight
Carrot Cake
Handmade Pistachio and Cinnamon Ice Cream
French Roast Coffee
Hazelnut Decaffeinated Coffee

Menu card from the 1997 Christmas Gala. The annual event raises money for Missouri Mansion Preservation and its restoration projects.

PUMPKIN CHEESECAKE

CRUST

- ¾ cup graham cracker crumbs
- ½ cup pecans, finely chopped
- ¼ cup light brown sugar, firmly packed
- ¼ cup sugar
- 4 tablespoons (½ stick) unsalted butter, melted and cooled

In a bowl combine the cracker crumbs, pecans, and sugars. Stir in butter and press the mixture into the bottom and ½ inch up the side of a buttered 9-inch springform pan. Chill crust for 1 hour before filling.

FILLING

- 1 ½ cups pumpkin
- 3 large eggs
- 1 ½ teaspoons cinnamon
- ½ teaspoon grated nutmeg
- ½ teaspoon ground ginger
- ½ teaspoon salt
- ½ cup light brown sugar, firmly packed
- 3 (8-ounce) packages cream cheese, cut in pieces
- ½ cup sugar
- 2 tablespoons whipping cream
- 1 tablespoon cornstarch
- 1 teaspoon vanilla
- 1 tablespoon bourbon (optional)

In a bowl, whisk together the pumpkin, eggs, cinnamon, nutmeg, ginger, salt, and brown sugar. Using an electric mixer, cream together the cream cheese and sugar. Add cream, cornstarch, vanilla, bourbon, and pumpkin mixture, beating until filling is smooth.

Pour filling into crust. Bake cheesecake in the middle of a preheated 350 degree oven for 50 to 55 minutes, or until center is set. Let cool in pan on a rack for 5 minutes.

Garnish with caramelized apple slices, pecans, or whipped cream.

Serves 8-10

Make individual tarts by pressing crust into a buttered, paper-lined baking tin and fill with pumpkin mixture. Bake at 300 degrees for 30 minutes.

State
Dinner

Governor Carnahan

ROOT VEGETABLE SOUP

4 tablespoons (½ stick) butter
3 large carrots, chopped
1 ½ cups leeks, white portion only, sliced
½ cup medium onion, chopped
½ teaspoon dried thyme
2 bay leaves
5 cups chicken broth
3 medium turnips, peeled, and chopped
   salt and pepper to taste
   fresh parsley
   bread croutons
   bacon bits

Melt butter in heavy saucepan over medium heat. Add carrots, leeks, onions, thyme, and bay leaves. Cover and cook until onions and leeks are translucent, stirring occasionally, about 12 minutes. Add chicken broth and turnips. Return cover and simmer until vegetables are very tender, about 35 minutes. Discard bay leaves. (Mixture can be chilled at this point, if making ahead.)

   Purée soup in batches in blender. Return to same saucepan and simmer, thinning with more broth, if desired. Season with salt and pepper. Ladle into bowls. Garnish with parsley, croutons, and/or bacon bits.

Serves 8

Selections from State
Dinner Menus

Root Vegetable Soup

Mixed Greens and
Hazelnut Encrusted Cheese
with Balsamic Vinaigrette

Sugar Snap Peas and
Baby Carrots

Talapia with White Wine
Sauce

Golden Risotto with
Asiago Cheese and
Sun-Dried Tomatoes

Whole Wheat Dinner
Loaves

Poached Pears with
Raspberries

Orange-Almond Biscotti

(Facing page) A bowl of Root Vegetable Soup served from the official china. (Right) The Great Seal of the State of Missouri.

MIXED GREENS AND HAZELNUT ENCRUSTED CHEESE
WITH BALSAMIC VINAIGRETTE

This vinaigrette is great with any green salad.

1 goat cheese log, about 11 ounces
¼ cup olive oil
¼ cup bread crumbs
¼ cup hazelnuts, ground
¾ pound mixed salad greens

Use dental floss to slice the cheese log cleanly. Pour oil into a shallow saucer and coat both sides of each cheese slice. Mix bread crumbs and ground hazelnuts; dip slices into mixture, coating both sides (this can be done ahead of time). Place coated cheese on baking sheet. Broil for 3 to 4 minutes or until crust turns deep golden. Transfer to dressed salad.

BALSAMIC VINAIGRETTE

2-3 garlic cloves, chopped
1 tablespoon honey mustard
2 tablespoons fresh lemon juice
3 tablespoons balsamic vinegar
½ cup olive oil
    salt and pepper to taste

Blend garlic, mustard, lemon juice, and vinegar in a food processor. Very slowly add oil and blend until desired consistency. Season with salt and pepper. Cover and chill. Return to room temperature and rewhisk before serving.

Dress salad and serve immediately. Refrigerate extra vinaigrette.

Serves 10-12

SUGAR SNAP PEAS AND BABY CARROTS

16-20   baby carrots, trimmed and peeled
  ¾   teaspoon salt
  1   tablespoon sugar
  ½   pound sugar snap peas, strings removed
  2   tablespoons (¼ stick) unsalted butter
  1   tablespoon garlic, minced
       salt and pepper

Fill skillet with enough water to measure ¾-inch deep. Bring to a boil and add carrots, salt, and sugar. Cook about 4 minutes or until crisp-tender. Add sugar snap peas and cook 1 minute; drain.

Plunge in large bowl of ice water to cool. Drain vegetables and pat dry.

Heat butter and garlic in skillet over high heat. Add vegetables. Stir fry about 2 minute or until warm through. Season with salt and pepper.

Serves 8

A tasty and decorative addition to any dinner plate.

A 1982 dinner menu during the administration of Governor Christopher "Kit" Bond and First Lady Carolyn Bond.

Talapia with White Wine Sauce, Golden Risotto,
and Sugar Snap Peas with Baby Carrots

TALAPIA WITH WHITE WINE SAUCE

1   cup flour
1   teaspoon salt
½   teaspoon pepper
4   (6-ounce) talapia filets
8   tablespoons (1 stick) butter
2   tablespoons chives, chopped
2   teaspoons parsley, chopped
¼   teaspoon Worcestershire sauce
½   teaspoon lemon peel, finely chopped
½   cup dry white wine
1   tablespoon lemon juice
½   cup heavy cream
1   teaspoon cornstarch
2   teaspoons water

Season flour with salt and pepper. Coat fish lightly and evenly in flour mixture and set aside. Heat butter in a large skillet until hot. Add fish, in batches, and cook over medium heat until done, about 4 minutes on each side.

In a small saucepan, heat chives, parsley, Worcestershire, lemon peel, wine, and lemon juice until reduced by one half. Add cream and bring to simmer. Add cornstarch that has been dissolved in water and cook one minute longer.

Divide fish onto plates; top with a small amount of sauce and serve.

Serves 4

This light, mild-flavored fish from the perch family gets rave reviews from Mansion guests.

GOLDEN RISOTTO
WITH ASIAGO CHEESE AND SUN-DRIED TOMATOES

6-8	cups canned or homemade chicken broth
6	tablespoons butter (¾ stick), divided
1	medium onion, finely chopped
2	cups arborio rice
¾	cup dry white wine
¼	cup sun-dried tomatoes, chopped
½	teaspoon saffron
¾	cup freshly grated Asiago cheese, divided
	salt to taste

Heat broth in medium saucepan. Meanwhile, melt 5 tablespoons of butter in large saucepan. When butter foams, add onions and sauté over medium heat. Add rice; mix well. Add wine and cook, stirring constantly until wine has evaporated.

Add ½ cup of the broth to the rice mixture and bring to a simmer, stirring constantly. When rice has absorbed the stock, add the remaining broth ½ cup at a time, stirring each time until rice has absorbed the liquid. Add sun-dried tomatoes before final addition of broth, reserving small amount of broth to dissolve saffron.

Continue cooking and stirring rice, about 15 to 20 minutes. Rice should be tender, but firm to the bite.

In a small bowl, dissolve saffron in a little hot broth and add to rice mixture. Stir in Asiago cheese, retaining enough to use as topping, and 1 tablespoon butter. Season with salt. Top with a sprinkle of Asiago cheese and serve. Or press rice into ½-cup buttered molds and invert onto plate.

Serves 6

The Missouri state flag adopted in 1913 features the Great Seal of the State of Missouri encircled by 24 stars denoting that Missouri was the 24th state to enter the Union.

WHOLE WHEAT DINNER LOAVES

2 packages of yeast
1 teaspoon sugar
½ cup warm water
1 cup milk, scalded
¾ cup shortening
2 eggs, beaten
¾ cup sugar
2 teaspoons salt
1 cup cold water
7 ½ cups whole wheat flour, or ½ white, ½ whole wheat mixture

Dissolve yeast and sugar in warm water. Scald milk in saucepan and add shortening to melt. Combine yeast and milk mixture in large mixing bowl. Add eggs, sugar, salt, and cold water.

Mix in flour and turn out on floured surface. Knead for 5 minutes. Let rise in warm place until double. Punch down and let rise again.

Shape into 2 loaves. Bake at 350 degrees for 35 minutes. Slice and serve warm.

Note: If a white bread is desired, substitute 7 ½ cups white flour for the whole wheat.

Yields 2 loaves

Nothing smells better than fresh home baked bread. This is a marvelous, foolproof recipe that produces a bread with a slightly sweet taste.

General George Custer (with rifle) and the Grand Duke Alexis of Russia were the first guests entertained in the present Mansion. In January 1872, the two men, who had been on a buffalo hunt in Nebraska, stopped in Jefferson City to have lunch at the Mansion with Governor and Mrs. B. Gratz Brown.

POACHED PEARS WITH RASPBERRIES

A light and elegant dessert.

4   large Anjou or Bosc pears, peeled and cored from bottom
1   bottle sweet blush wine
½   cup sugar
1   teaspoon vanilla
1   cinnamon stick
1   cup whipping cream, whipped (optional)
1   cup raspberries (optional)

Cut a thick slice from the bottom of each pear so that they stand upright. Leave stems intact. In a saucepan, mix the wine, sugar, and vanilla. Place pears bottom side down in sauce with liquid reaching half way up the pears. Simmer until pears are soft. Cool pears in the sauce for about one hour. Remove pears with slotted spoon.

Place sauce back over medium heat and reduce to syrup consistency. Paint bottom of plate with sauce. Garnish with dot of whipped cream. Run toothpick through cream to make a web pattern in sauce. Place pear in middle of plate. Garnish with raspberries.

Serves 4

ORANGE-ALMOND BISCOTTI

This homebaked biscotti is noticeably softer than the commerical varieties.

2   cups flour
1   cup sugar
1   teaspoon baking soda
¼   teaspoon salt
3   eggs, plus 1 egg yolk, divided
1   teaspoon vanilla
1   tablespoon orange zest
1 ½ cups almonds, whole, toasted then chopped coarse
1   teaspoon water

Blend flour, sugar, soda, and salt. In a small bowl, whisk together 2 eggs, yolk, vanilla, and zest; add to flour mixture. Stir in almonds. Turn dough onto lightly floured surface; knead several times and halve dough. Working with floured hands on a large buttered and floured baking sheet, form each dough half into a flattish log 12 inches long and 2 inches wide. Place logs 3 inches apart on the sheet. Brush with egg wash made from 1 beaten egg and water.

Bake logs at 325 degrees for 20 minutes; remove. Reduce oven to 300 degrees. Cool logs on baking rack for 10 minutes. On a cutting board, slice logs crosswise into ½-inch-wide slices. Arrange biscotti, cut side down, on baking sheet and bake for another 5 minutes on each side, or until pale golden. Transfer biscotti to racks to cool. Biscotti will keep in airtight containers for 3 days.

Yields 48

Poached Pears with Raspberries

Legislative
Dinner

FIELD GREENS AND COCONUT SHRIMP

20-24 large shrimp (3 per salad), peeled and deveined
   1 egg
   1 teaspoon seasoned salt
   ¾ cup beer
1 ¼ cups flour
     vegetable oil
   2 (7-ounce) packages shredded coconut
   ¾ pound mixed salad greens

Cut shrimp in half lengthwise and set aside. Combine egg, seasoned salt, and beer. Gradually stir in flour, beating till smooth. Pour 1 ½ inches of oil into a large skillet and bring to medium-high temperature, about 325 degrees.

   Put coconut in a shallow bowl. Dip shrimp in batter, then coat with coconut. Fry a few at a time for about 4 minutes, or until golden on both sides. Drain on paper towels.

   Dress salad with your favorite dressing (or Basil Vinaigrette, page 54). Place three shrimp around edge of salad just before serving.

   If preparing ahead, refrigerate shrimp after frying and reheat the next day in a preheated 350 degree oven for about 5 minutes.

Serves 12

Menu Selections from
Legislative Dinners
1992-1999

Field Greens and Coconut
Shrimp

Turkey Medallion
Florentine

Julienne Carrots and
Zucchini

Crusty Potato Galette

Garlic Parmesan Bread

Rum Raisin Apple Pie
with Flaky Pie Crust

Cinnamon Ice Cream

(Facing page) The State Capitol in Jefferson City houses the offices and legislative chambers for Missouri's 34 state senators and 163 house members. (Right) Field Greens and Coconut Shrimp.

TURKEY MEDALLION FLORENTINE

May be prepared a day ahead and refrigerated until ready to cook.

1 tablespoon seasoned salt
1 teaspoon salt
½ teaspoon black pepper
1 teaspoon garlic powder
6 (6-ounce) bacon-wrapped turkey tenderloins

Mix seasonings and sprinkle on both sides of turkey medallions. Place medallions in a very hot grill pan and cook for 1 minute; rotate a quarter turn and cook for 1 minute more. Turn meat over and repeat. Remove turkey from grill pan and place in baking dish. Cook in a preheated 350 degree oven for 20 minutes.

SAUCE

1 tablespoon butter
2 garlic cloves, minced
2 cups whipping cream
1 (10-ounce) package frozen chopped spinach, thawed
1 ½ teaspoons chicken bouillon granules
1 tablespoon cornstarch dissolved in 2 tablespoons water
   salt and pepper to taste

Melt butter in a saucepan; sauté garlic until soft but not brown. Add cream, spinach, and chicken bouillon granules. Bring to a slow boil and simmer for about 10 to 15 minutes. Add dissolved cornstarch slowly to form a smooth sauce.

   Salt and pepper to taste. Place small amount of spinach mixture on serving plate and top with turkey medallion.

Serves 6

Turkey Medallion Florentine, Crusty Potato Galette, and Julienne Carrots and Zucchini

JULIENNE CARROTS AND ZUCCHINI

2   medium carrots
1   zucchini squash
1   yellow squash

2   tablespoons (¼ stick) butter or olive oil
1   clove garlic, finely chopped
     salt and pepper to taste

Cut carrots and squash into matchstick-size pieces. Heat oil; add garlic and cook for 30 seconds. Add carrots and cook 3 minutes more, stirring frequently. Add squash and cook another 3 minutes. Add salt and pepper.

Serves 6

CRUSTY POTATO GALETTE

4 tablespoons (½ stick) unsalted butter, melted
4 tablespoons vegetable oil
3 pounds potatoes, unpeeled
¾ teaspoon salt
¾ teaspoon pepper
½ cup Parmesan cheese

In a small bowl, stir together butter and oil. Slice the potatoes very thinly, about ⅛-inch thick. Brush the bottom of a 9-inch cast-iron skillet with some of the butter mixture; cover it with a layer of potato slices, overlapping edges.

Brush the potatoes with some of the remaining butter mixture; sprinkle with salt, pepper, and Parmesan cheese. Repeat layers until all slices are used.

Heat the skillet over moderately high heat until it begins to sizzle. Transfer skillet to the middle of a preheated 450 degree oven and bake galette for 45 minutes, or until golden and potatoes are tender. Let cool for 15 minutes and cut into wedges. Remove with spatula to plate or platter.

Serves 6-8

For an extra treat, slip thin slices of Golden Delicious apple between one of the potato layers before cooking.

GARLIC PARMESAN BREAD

1 loaf French bread
1 stick unsalted butter
2 cloves garlic, mashed
¼ cup fresh dill, finely chopped
¼ cup fresh Parmigiano-Reggiano cheese, grated

Slice bread lengthwise. Melt butter in a small skillet. Add garlic and heat for 2 minutes. Brush the melted butter on the cut sides of the bread halves. Sprinkle with dill and cheese.

Bake in a 375 degree oven until golden, about 5 to 8 minutes. Cut each half crosswise into 1-inch slices and serve immediately.

Serves 6-8

A crusty loaf enhanced by the flavor of garlic, dill, and Parmesan cheese.

FLAKY PIE CRUST

1 ¾ cup flour

1 teaspoon salt

10 tablespoons (1 ¼ sticks) chilled unsalted butter,
        cut lengthwise and into ⅜-inch pieces

2 tablespoons chilled shortening

5-8 tablespoons ice water

In medium bowl, combine flour and salt. By hand, rub in butter and shortening until it is the size of cornflakes (or cut in with pastry blender). Add ice water a tablespoon at a time. Form dough into ball and chill at least 1 hour. Divide dough in half and roll out on lightly floured surface.

Yields 2 large pie crusts

Interior view of the Missouri Capitol dome.

RUM RAISIN APPLE PIE

A delicious twist on traditional apple pie.

⅓ cup raisins
2 tablespoons dark rum
½ cup brown sugar, packed lightly
3 tablespoons flour
¾ teaspoon ground cinnamon
¼ teaspoon freshly grated nutmeg
¼ teaspoon grated lemon peel
¼ teaspoon salt
2 ½ pounds Golden Delicious apples, peeled and cored
2 teaspoons fresh lemon juice
pastry dough for double crust 9-inch pie
¾ cup chopped pecans
2 tablespoons (¼ stick) cold unsalted butter, cut into pieces
1 tablespoon milk
1 ½ teaspoons sugar

Combine raisins and rum in a small saucepan and simmer over medium heat. Remove pan and let raisins stand for 10 minutes or until liquid is absorbed.

In a large bowl, combine brown sugar, flour, cinnamon, nutmeg, lemon peel, and salt. Slice apples thinly and add to brown sugar mixture. Add raisins and lemon juice. Stir well.

Mound apple mixture in prepared pie shell, sprinkle with pecans, and dot with butter. Cover with top crust and crimp edges to seal. Cut vent in top crust. Brush with milk and sprinkle with sugar.

Bake at 425 degrees for 30 minutes. Reduce to 375 degrees and bake 20 to 25 minutes more or until apples are tender. Cool on rack. Serve at room temperature with ice cream.

Serves 6-8

CINNAMON ICE CREAM

4 cups milk
1 cup sugar
½ cup honey
¼ teaspoon salt
6 eggs, well beaten
4 cups whipping cream, chilled
2 teaspoons vanilla
2 teaspoons cinnamon

In a saucepan, combine milk, sugar, honey, and salt. Whisk until smooth. Cook over medium heat, bringing to a gentle boil. Cook until mixture is thick enough to coat metal spoon with thin film, about 160 degrees.

In a small mixing bowl, whisk eggs together. Add 1 cup of hot liquid to egg mixture, whisking until smooth. Whisk egg mixture back into hot cream. Continue cooking for 4 minutes. Remove from heat and cool completely.

When ready to freeze, add cream, vanilla, and cinnamon to custard. Pour into 5- to 6-quart electric ice cream freezer container and process according to directions, using 6 parts ice to 1 part rock salt.

Yields 4 quarts

The honey helps makes this a smooth frozen custard.

(Right) Statue of President Thomas Jefferson at the south entrance to the Capitol. Jefferson instigated the Louisiana Purchase from which the state of Missouri was later formed.

79

Docents' Luncheon

Red Pepper and Potato Combo

Red Pepper Soup

3 medium red bell peppers, thinly sliced
2 tablespoons olive oil
1 medium onion, sliced
1 garlic clove, finely chopped
½ cup dry white wine
½ teaspoon salt
¼ teaspoon cayenne
4 cups chicken broth
1 cup half-and-half cream
¼ cup flour

Charbroil peppers in oven until blackened on all sides. Enclose in a small bag and let stand 10 minutes. Peel, seed, and slice.

Heat olive oil in large heavy saucepan. Add onion and cook over medium heat for 5 minutes, or until soft. Add the red peppers and garlic. Continue to cook for 5 minutes, stirring occasionally. Add the white wine and cook over moderate heat for about 5 minutes, until wine is reduced so that it just covers the bottom of the pan. Sprinkle with salt and cayenne.

Stir in chicken broth and bring mixture to a boil. Reduce heat and cover. Simmer for 10 to 12 minutes or until vegetables are soft. Cool slightly and strain into saucepan, retaining vegetables.

Purée the vegetables in a blender and return to saucepan. In a medium bowl, gradually whisk cream into flour. Slowly whisk mixture into soup. Continue whisking the soup over moderately high heat until it boils and thickens.

Prepare Potato Soup on following page.

(Facing page) Fifty costumed docents serve as tour guides on Tuesdays and Thursdays when the Mansion is open to the public.
(Right) More than 58,000 people visit the Victorian home each year.

A Docents' Luncheon
Menu

Red Pepper and Potato
Combo

Curried Chicken Salad

Corn Muffins

Orange Soufflé

Red Pepper and Potato Combo

POTATO SOUP

1 pound russet potatoes, peeled and cut into chunks	½ teaspoon white pepper
	½ pound leeks, white part only, sliced, divided
3 cups water	1 ½ tablespoons olive oil
2 teaspoons salt	1 teaspoon soy sauce
1 bay leaf	1 ⅓ cups chicken stock or bouillon (if bouillon, reduce salt)
¾ teaspoon dried oregano	½ cup whipping cream
¾ teaspoon dried thyme	1 ½ cups half-and-half cream
	2 tablespoons chopped scallions or chives

Place potatoes in a large pot along with the water, salt, herbs, spices, and half the leeks. Cook over medium heat.

Cook the remaining leeks in olive oil for 10 to 15 minutes, stirring frequently. Add soy sauce after leeks begin to caramelize. Continue cooking until leeks are caramel in color, but not crispy or black.

Add stock or bouillon to leek mixture and combine with potato pot, being careful to include all drippings from pan. When potatoes are soft, remove pot from burner and remove bay leaf. Process the soup in a blender until pureed. Return soup to pot and whisk in whipping cream and half-and-half cream. Bring soup to gentle boil.

Remove from heat and serve by pouring Potato Soup and the Red Pepper Soup into a bowl simultaneously to form a two-color soup. Garnish with scallions or chives.

Serves 6-8

CURRIED CHICKEN SALAD

2   cups cooked chicken breasts, diced
4   scallions, sliced
1   cup water chestnuts, sliced
2   cups cooked rice, at room temperature
1   cup mayonnaise
½   cup mango chutney
1   teaspoon curry powder, or to taste
1   teaspoon salt
    freshly ground pepper to taste
2   bananas
¼   cup lemon juice
1 ½   cups chopped peanuts

Combine chicken, scallions, and water chestnuts with rice.
In a separate bowl combine mayonnaise, chutney, curry, salt, and
pepper; mix well. Thoroughly combine mayonnaise dressing with
chicken-rice mixture; chill. Taste and adjust seasonings.

Cut bananas diagonally into 1-inch slices. Dip into lemon juice
and coat with peanuts. To serve, arrange salad on small platter.
Surround salad with coated banana slices and garnish with
additional chopped nuts.

Note: Pass condiments—chopped green peppers, toasted
almonds, raisins, and coconut.

Serves 6-8

*An update of an old
favorite from an earlier
Mansion cookbook,
Past & Repast.*

Costumed docents give guided
tours of the 1871 home—one of the
finest Victorian restorations in the
country.

Corn Muffins

Bursting with flavor, these muffins will please your family and guests anytime.

6 tablespoons (¾ stick) butter or margarine, divided
2 ears fresh corn
¼ cup onion, finely chopped
1 cup all-purpose flour
1 cup yellow cornmeal
1 ½ teaspoons baking powder
½ teaspoon baking soda
1 teaspoon salt
2 tablespoons sugar
1 cup buttermilk
1 large egg
1 cup (4 ounces) cheddar cheese, shredded
1 (4.5-ounce) can chopped green chilies, drained
¼ cup sunflower kernels (optional)

Melt 2 tablespoons butter in a large skillet over medium-high heat. Cut corn from cob and add to skillet along with onion. Cook until tender, stirring often.

Combine flour and next 5 ingredients in large bowl. Make a well in center of mixture.

Combine buttermilk, egg, and 4 tablespoons melted butter. Add to dry ingredients, stirring just until moistened. Stir in corn mixture, cheese, and chilies. Spoon into 12 lightly greased muffin cups, filling each three-fourths full. Sprinkle with sunflower kernels, if desired.

Bake at 375 degrees for 18 to 20 minutes or until muffins are golden. Remove from pan immediately and cool on wire racks.

Yields 1 dozen

Orange Soufflé

3 tablespoons butter
¼ cup flour
  dash salt
⅔ cup milk
1 teaspoon orange peel, finely shredded
⅓ cup orange juice
4 egg yolks
4 egg whites
¼ cup sugar

In a small saucepan, melt butter; stir in flour and salt. Add milk and cook, stirring until thick and bubbly. Remove from heat; stir in orange peel and juice. In a small mixer bowl, beat egg yolks about 5 minutes or until thick and lemon colored. Gradually stir orange mixture into beaten egg yolks. Wash beaters thoroughly.

Using an electric mixer, beat egg whites until soft peaks form. Gradually add sugar, beating until whites form stiff peaks. Fold orange mixture into egg whites.

Attach a buttered and sugared foil collar to a 2-quart soufflé dish. Turn mixture into dish, or ramekins if making individual portions. If using ramekins, brush each with softened butter and fill with granulated sugar, shaking out any excess. Fill the dish or ramekins to within ¼ inch of the rim. (Filling will rise above the rim as it bakes.) Bake in a 325 degree oven for 60 to 65 minutes, or until golden in color. (If using ramekins, bake about 45 minutes.)

Serve immediately with Orange Sauce or dust with powdered sugar.

Yields 6 servings

Orange Sauce

½ cup sugar
2 tablespoons cornstarch
  dash of salt

1 ½ cups orange juice
1 tablespoon butter

Combine all ingredients in a medium saucepan. Cook and stir until thick and bubbly. Cook 2 minutes more. Remove from heat; stir in butter. Drizzle warm sauce lightly over soufflé.

Yields 1 ¾ cups

Cook this wonderful, light dessert in a soufflé dish or individual ramekins.

Secretaries' Luncheon

CRUNCHY ROMAINE TOSS

1   package ramen noodles, crumbled
1   cup walnuts, chopped
4   tablespoons (½ stick) butter
½   cup oil
¼   cup wine vinegar
⅓   cup sugar
1 ½   teaspoons soy sauce
    salt and pepper to taste
1   head romaine lettuce, chopped
1   bunch broccoli, chopped into small pieces
4   green onions, chopped

Lay aside seasoning packet from ramen noodles. Mix walnuts, butter, and noodles in baking dish and brown for 10 minutes or more in a 350 degree oven. Cool ingredients on paper towel.

For the dressing, combine oil, vinegar, sugar, soy sauce, salt, and pepper in a jar. Shake well. Combine dressing and noodles with the lettuce, broccoli, and onions. Toss well and serve immediately.

Serves 8

A Secretaries' Luncheon Menu

Crunchy Romaine Toss

Cashew Chicken

Mandarin Stir-Fried Rice

Fresh Fruit Compote with Zabaglione Sauce

Vanilla Butter Buttons

(Right) From the earliest days of the Mansion, the five-foot-tall bronze Newel Post Lady—perched on the post at the foot of the stairs—greeted all those who climbed or slid down the Grand Stairway. She was removed during a remodeling in the late 1930s, but in 1995 she was replaced by another statue nearly identical to the original.

Cashew Chicken

A wonderful combination of flavors.

4 chicken breast halves, boned and skinned
1 ½ cups flour
3 eggs, beaten well
¾ cup milk
¼ teaspoon salt
  pinch of pepper
  unsalted cashews
  sliced green onions

Cut chicken into 1x1½-inch pieces. Dredge in flour; let stand 15 minutes.

Combine eggs, milk, salt, and pepper. Place chicken in egg mixture, and let stand 10 minutes. Dredge chicken again in flour. Fry chicken pieces in deep hot oil (375 degrees) 3 to 5 minutes, or until golden brown.

Spoon sauce over chicken; top with cashews and onions. Sprinkle with soy sauce, if desired. Serve over rice.

Yields 4-5 servings

Sauce

1 ½ cups chicken broth, divided
3 tablespoons cornstarch
1 ½ teaspoons sugar
3 teaspoons oyster sauce

Pour 1 cup broth into a small saucepan. Stir cornstarch into remaining broth. Add cornstarch mixture, sugar, and oyster sauce to broth. Cook over low heat, stirring constantly, until thick and bubbly.

Yields 1 ½ cups

MANDARIN STIR-FRIED RICE

6 tablespoons peanut oil for cooking, divided
2 eggs, beaten with a pinch of salt (optional)
2 tablespoons green onions, chopped
1 teaspoon fresh garlic, finely chopped
6 cups cooked cold rice
½ cup small shrimp (optional)
½ cup ham, diced
½ cup frozen green peas
1 tablespoon rice wine
1 tablespoon soy sauce
1 tablespoon sesame oil
pepper to taste

Heat 2 tablespoons of peanut oil in wok. Stir fry eggs for 5 seconds and remove from wok. Heat 3 to 4 tablespoons oil in wok; add chopped green onions and garlic. Cook a few seconds. Add cold rice and stir fry 3 minutes. Add shrimp, ham, peas, and rice wine; warm thoroughly. Return eggs to wok. Blend and season with soy sauce, sesame oil, and pepper to taste.

Serves 6

A friend from Taiwan introduced me to this recipe for her family's favorite rice dish.

FRESH FRUIT COMPOTE
WITH ZABAGLIONE SAUCE

Fresh fruit is a pleasant finale to any meal.

1 medium banana, peeled and sliced
1 teaspoon lemon juice
1 small apple, cored and cut into thin wedges
1 medium-size orange, peeled, sliced crosswise and seeded
1 medium pear, cored and cut into thin wedges
½ cup seedless red grapes, halved
2 kiwi, peeled and sliced
½ cup seedless green grapes, halved
½ pint fresh strawberries, hulled and halved
¾ cup Champagne or orange juice

Sprinkle banana slices with lemon juice. Combine with other fruits in a large bowl. Add Champagne or orange juice; chill for 1 hour. Strain and spoon into stemmed compotes. Serve with a light topping of Zabaglione Sauce.

Yields 10 servings

ZABAGLIONE SAUCE

8 egg yolks
1 cup granulated sugar
½ cup dry Marsala wine
orange zest
fresh mint leaves

This classic Zabaglione (pronounced: zah-bahl-YOH-nay) has been described as one of Italy's great gifts to world cuisine.

Using an electric mixer, beat egg yolks and sugar until pale and thick. Transfer to the top of a double boiler over simmering water; do not let water boil. Add wine slowly, beating constantly.
The mixture will triple in volume and become light and fluffy in about 4 to 6 minutes.

Chill over bowl of ice water, continuing to stir until cool. Spoon lightly onto the Fresh Fruit Compote (or berries, if desired) and garnish with mint. Zabaglione Sauce can be made a day ahead and refrigerated.

Serves 4-6

Fresh Fruit Compote

VANILLA BUTTER BUTTONS

12 tablespoons (1 ½ sticks) unsalted butter
⅓ cup sugar
1 egg

1 teaspoon vanilla
¾ cup flour

Preheat oven to 350 degrees. Cream butter and sugar on low speed using an electric mixer. Add egg and vanilla; continue to mix. Gradually add flour, mixing well. Using a pastry bag with a ½-inch tip, pipe ½-inch balls of dough 1 inch apart onto parchment paper-lined cookie sheets. Bake one tray at a time, rotating the tray after 5 minutes. Bake 5 minutes more or until the cookies are brown on the edges and set in the center. (Watch carefully since these cookies quickly become too brown.) Let cool before removing from sheets. Serve with the Fresh Fruit Compote or refrigerate in airtight tins.

If desired, cookies can be sandwiched together with a thin filling made by combining 4 ounces semisweet chocolate chips, 1 tablespoon softened butter or margarine, 1 tablespoon Grand Marnier, and 2 tablespoons orange zest.

Yields more than 100 tiny unfilled cookies

Afternoon Tea

PUMPKIN PECAN BREAD

- 4 large eggs, lightly beaten
- 1 (16-ounce) can pumpkin
- 2 cups sugar
- ¾ cup vegetable oil
- ⅔ cup water
- 2 teaspoons vanilla extract
- 3 ⅓ cups all-purpose flour
- 2 teaspoons baking soda
- ½ teaspoon baking powder
- ¾ teaspoon salt
- 2 teaspoons pumpkin pie spice
- 1 teaspoon ground nutmeg
- 1 teaspoon ground cinnamon
- 1 cup pecans, chopped

Combine first 6 ingredients in a large bowl. Stir well. Combine flour and next 6 ingredients. Add flour mixture to pumpkin mixture, stirring to blend. Stir in pecans.

Spoon batter into 2 greased 9x5x3-inch loaf pans. Bake at 350 degrees for 50 to 60 minutes, or until pick inserted in center comes out clean. Cool in pans on wire rack for 10 minutes. Remove from pans and let cool completely on wire racks.

Yields 2 loaves

A graceful cup,
a dainty napkin,
a silver spoon,
a lace doily,
a cherished tea set.
Tea is a sip of yesterday.

Tea Time Favorites

Pumpkin Pecan Bread

Tea Sandwiches

Currant and Orange Scones
with Orange Butter

Black Walnut-Apple Bars

Victorian Spiced Tea Punch

Mini-Cheesecakes

Strawberry Bonnets

Lemon Tea Bread

Christmas Almond Bars

Chocolate-Covered Cherry Cookies

Cashew Cookies

Coconut Bread

Mint Brownies

Cran-Apple Tartlets

Featherlight Chocolate Chip Cookies

"Please Come to Tea"

"There are few hours in life more agreeable than the hour dedicated to the ceremony know as afternoon tea." ~Henry James

A crackling fire, quiet music, and the gentle chink of china cups traditionally set the stage for a relaxed afternoon tea with friends. Accompanied by small cakes and scones, the tasty brew was most often served from a tray or cart in the parlor, garden, or on the patio. By contrast, British high tea was a sit-down meal served later in the day when the man of the house returned from work.

But the 19th century writer Samuel Johnson felt that any hour or place was good for tea. He declared: "[I am] a hardened and shameless tea drinker, who has for twenty years diluted his meals with only the infusion of this fascinating plant; whose kettle has scarcely time to cool; who with tea amuses the evening, with tea solaces the midnight, and with tea welcomes the morning." Today's wide range of blends makes tea drinking an even more adventuresome and pleasurable pastime.

The Perfect Cup of Tea

1. Start with fresh, cold tap water.
2. Bring the water to a full boil over high heat.
3. Select a good quality tea.
4. Temper the tea pot by filling with hot water before using. Pour out water.
5. Fill a tea ball or infuser with loose tea, allowing one teaspoon for each cup of water and one for the pot. If using tea bags, allow one bag per cup.
6. Be sure the water is as near the boiling point as possible when it is poured over the tea.
7. Allow the tea to steep 3 minutes, or up to 5 minutes if using milk.
8. The rule on adding milk comes from tea expert Angela Hynes. "Adding milk before tea was originally just a means of protecting the delicate bone china teacups from the hot tea, though some people also swear it makes a difference in the taste by taking the edge off the tannin."
9. Serve from your best china cups. Offer sliced lemon and sugar. Cloth napkins and a few flowers in a small vase will also enhance the pleasure of a tea party.

Tea for Large Parties

Make tea as directed on package, but use 1 quart (4 cups) of water over ⅔ cup of tea leaves. Let stand 5 minutes, then stir and strain into teapot or pitcher. Use an earthenware or glass pot, as metal distorts the flavor of the tea. When ready to serve, pour about 2 tablespoons of concentrate into each cup, then fill with hot water. This will serve 25 cups.

When using tea bags, avoid squeezing or wringing the bag into the cup as this will cause a bitter residue in the tea. Do not use a tea bag twice; all the flavor is exhausted in the first infusion.

You are going out to tea today,
So mind how you behave;
Let all accounts I have of you
Be pleasant ones, I crave.

Don't spill your tea, or gnaw your bread,
And don't tease one another;
And Tommy musn't talk too much
Or quarrel with his brother.

Say, "If you please," and "thank you Nurse,"
Come home at eight o'clock;
And Fanny, pray, be careful that
You do not tear your frock.

Now, mind your manners, children five,
Attend to what I say;
And then, perhaps, I'll let you go
Again another day.

"Under the Window"
~Kate Greenaway, 1877

A tea party at the Mansion is a new experience
for Zoë Bednar and Imani Taylor.

CHOOSING A TEA

Assam: A brisk, India tea with a malty aroma. Great for a morning wake up.

Chamomile: A light, soothing drink thought to aid digestion and relaxation. Good with honey.

Ceylon: A golden-colored, high quality tea best served with lemon or milk. Serve anytime.

Darjeeling: Known as the "Champagne of Tea." A wonderful, rich flavored brew with a nutty quality associated with Muscat grapes.

Earl Grey: A blend of Darjeeling and China teas flavored with oil of bergamot. A delicate afternoon tea best served without milk or lemon. It is named after a 19th century British prime minister.

English Breakfast: A robust, morning tea. Best served with milk and sugar.

Formosa Oolong: An expensive, high quality tea producing a pale yellow brew with a subtle peach flavor. Serve without milk as an afternoon or evening tea.

Keemun: A tea for meal time. Often used for breakfast blends.

Prince of Wales: This popular afternoon tea is a blend of Keemun teas that was created for the Duke of Windsor.

Pekoe and Orange Pekoe: This label is used today to designate the size of the tea leaf, not the flavor. Pekoe describes the largest grade of tea, as opposed to broken pekoe, the smaller fannings, and the even smaller fines.

TEA SANDWICHES

Trim crusts from very thin slices of white and wheat sandwich bread. Spread each slice lightly with softened butter. Spread about 1 ½ tablespoons of one of the fillings evenly to edges of half of bread slices. Cover with other half of bread slices.

Cut into squares, triangles, or cut with holiday-shaped cookie cutters. Arrange on serving trays; cover with wax paper, slightly dampened tea towel, and plastic wrap. Refrigerate several hours until ready to serve.

CHICKEN CHUTNEY WITH SMOKED ALMONDS

In medium bowl, combine your favorite chicken salad (or use half pint deli chicken spread) combined with 2 tablespoons chutney and ¼ teaspoon curry powder. Spread to form sandwiches and cut into 2-inch rounds, making 48 tea-sized sandwiches. Put ½ cup finely chopped smoked almonds or cashews on a small plate. Spread a light coat of mayonnaise along edges of sandwiches and roll edges in nuts.

HAM-PINEAPPLE FILLING WITH HONEY BUTTER

In food processor, blend 1 cup chopped ham, ½ cup fresh chopped pineapple or drained canned pineapple, 1 teaspoon Dijon mustard, and pepper to taste. Blend 2 sticks of butter with 2 tablespoons of honey and spread on 20 thin slices of whole wheat bread. Top with ham mixture and additional 20 slices of bread. Cut into triangles or shapes with cookie cutter.

SALMON WITH MUSTARD SAUCE

Place thin slices of salmon atop rectangular cut pumpernickel or wheat bread. Place a small dollop of Mustard Sauce on salmon and garnish with a small dill sprig. For Mustard Sauce, whisk together ½ cup vegetable oil, ½ cup plain nonfat yogurt, ¼ cup coarse-grained mustard, ½ cup lime juice, and salt and pepper to taste.

CURRANT AND ORANGE SCONES
WITH ORANGE BUTTER

  3   cups flour
  ⅓   cup sugar
2 ½   teaspoons baking powder
  ½   teaspoon baking soda
 12   tablespoons (1 ½ sticks) cold butter, cut into cubes
  ⅓   cup currants
  1   cup buttermilk
  1   tablespoon grated orange zest
  1   tablespoon milk

Fruit-laced scones reminiscent of the traditional English tea time favorites.

Combine first 4 ingredients in a medium-sized bowl. Add butter. Using your fingers, work the butter into the flour mixture until it resembles cornmeal (some large lumps can remain). Add currants.

 Add buttermilk and orange zest. Stir with a fork just until moist. Gather dough into a ball and knead gently on a lightly floured surface, about 3 to 4 times. Pat the dough into a circle about ¾-inch thick. Cut out scones with a medium-sized biscuit cutter. Lift the cookie cutter straight up when cutting or scones will be lopsided. Brush with milk. Place on an ungreased cookie sheet and bake at 450 degrees 12 to 15 minutes, or until barely golden. Serve with orange marmalade.

 Note: The secret to flaky scones is to use cold butter and to handle the dough as little as possible. The dough should be rough, not smooth. Pat, rather than roll, the dough into shape.

Yields 18 scones

ORANGE BUTTER

In a small bowl combine 8 tablespoons (1 stick) softened butter or margarine, 1 teaspoon grated orange peel, and 1 tablespoon powdered sugar. Beat until creamy and smooth. Serve with warm scones.

 Note: Lemon curd and clotted cream (or Devonshire cream) often accompanies these light tender biscuits served in English tea shops. While true clotted cream is hard to find in the U.S., you can make lemon curd yourself or purchase it in specialty shops.

Black Walnut-Apple Bars

Missouri's abundance of black walnut trees and renown apple orchards makes this a favorite "Show-Me State" cookie.

½ cup all-purpose flour
½ cup sugar
1 teaspoon baking powder
1 teaspoon ground cinnamon
¼ teaspoon salt
1 egg
1 teaspoon vanilla extract
1 cup apple, chopped
¼ cup black walnuts, chopped
¼ cup powdered sugar, sifted
2 teaspoons hot water
⅛ teaspoon black walnut-flavored extract

Combine first 5 ingredients in a large bowl, mixing well. Add egg and vanilla; stir until blended. Stir in apple and nuts. Coat 8-inch-square pan with cooking spray and pour in batter. Bake at 400 degrees for 15 to 20 minutes, or until a wooden pick inserted in center comes out clean. Cool on a wire rack. Combine powdered sugar, water, and extract; stir until smooth for glaze. Drizzle top with glaze; cut into 2x1-inch bars.

Yields 32 bars

Victorian Spiced Tea Punch

Tea is a natural source of antioxidants that help to maintain healthy cells and tissues. It contains no calories, fat, or sugar.

1 teaspoon whole cloves
2 sticks whole cinnamon
6 quarts cold water
5 teaspoons black tea (or 5 tea bags)
    juice of 6 oranges, about 1 cup
    juice of 3 lemons, about ½ cup
1 ½ cups pineapple juice
1 ½ cups sugar (or use sweetener of equal strength)

Place spices in a cheesecloth or tea-infusion bag. Place tea in a separate bag, if using loose tea. Bring water to a boil and add tea and spices. Let stand 5 minutes; remove and discard bags. Stir in the juices, sugar, or sweetener, adjusting to taste. Serve hot or cold.

Yields 35 punch cups

MINI-CHEESECAKES

1 ½ cups graham cracker or chocolate wafer crumbs
 ¼ cup sugar
 4 tablespoons (½ stick) margarine or butter, melted
 3 (8-ounce) packages cream cheese, softened
 1 (14-ounce) can sweetened condensed milk
 3 eggs
 2 teaspoons vanilla extract

Preheat oven to 300 degrees. Line mini-muffin tins with paper
cups. Combine crumbs, sugar, and margarine; press equal portions
into bottoms of tins. In large mixer bowl, beat cheese until fluffy.
Gradually beat in sweetened condensed milk until smooth.
Add eggs and vanilla; mix well.

Spoon mixture into tins, filling each cup ¾ full. Bake 20 minutes
or until cakes spring back when lightly touched. Chill. Garnish as
desired with fruit pieces, such as mandarin oranges or kiwis.

Note: If greased muffin tins are used instead of paper-lined tins,
cool baked cheesecakes and put in freezer for 15 minutes before
removing from tins.

Yields 24 cakes

Luscious morsels of cheesecake to highlight your tea party.

First Lady Jerry Dalton (right corner)
visits with her guests in the double
parlor during a 1960s tea party.

(Clockwise from upper right) Strawberry Bonnets; Chicken Chutney Tea Sandwiches, Coconut Bread, Pumpkin Pecan Bread, Cran-Apple Tartlets, Cashew Cookies, and Chocolate-Covered Cherry Cookies

STRAWBERRY BONNETS

20 large fresh strawberries, divided
1 (3-ounce) package cream cheese, softened
2 tablespoons walnuts or pecans, finely chopped

1 ½ tablespoons powdered sugar
1 teaspoon orange liqueur or milk

Dice 2 strawberries and set aside. Cut a thin slice from stem end of remaining strawberries, forming a base. Cut each berry into four wedges, starting at pointed ends and cutting toward base, but not through it.

Beat cream cheese at medium speed with an electric mixer until fluffy. Stir in diced strawberries, nuts, powdered sugar, and orange liqueur or milk. Spoon about 1 teaspoon or less of mixture into each strawberry.

Yields 18 berries

LEMON TEA BREAD

3 cups flour
2 teaspoons baking powder
½ teaspoon salt
12 tablespoons (1 ½ sticks) unsalted butter, softened
2 cups sugar
2 teaspoons lemon zest, finely grated
4 large eggs
1 cup whole milk
2 teaspoons poppy seeds
1 tablespoon fresh lemon juice

A lemon lovers delight!

Preheat oven to 325 degrees. Butter and flour two 9x5x3-inch metal loaf pans, or 5 mini-loaf pans (6x6x2 inches). Shake out excess flour.

In a mixing bowl, sift together flour, baking powder, and salt. Using an electric mixer, beat together butter, sugar, and zest until light and fluffy. Beat in eggs one at a time, beating well after each addition.

With mixer on low speed, add flour mixture and milk alternately, beginning and ending with flour mixture. Beat just until batter is combined well. Beat in poppy seeds and lemon juice.

Divide batter between loaf pans, smoothing tops. Bake loaves in middle of a 325 degree oven, or until a pick comes out clean, about 1 hour.

Cool loaves in pans on a wire rack 15 minutes. Run a thin knife around edges of pans and invert loaves onto rack. Turn loaves right side up and pierce tops all over with a thin skewer or toothpick. Repeatedly brush Lemon Glaze over tops of loaves until all glaze is absorbed.

Note: If using small bread pans, bake for about 45 minutes. Tea bread keeps for 4 days wrapped in foil or airtight container at room temperature. Can be frozen.

Yields 2 loaves

LEMON GLAZE

⅓ cup fresh lemon juice
½ cup sugar

While loaves are baking, prepare glaze by stirring together lemon juice and sugar until sugar is dissolved.

CHRISTMAS ALMOND BARS

Wonderful for tea or
dessert any time of year.

1   cup sugar
8   tablespoons (1 stick) butter or margarine, softened
1   egg
½   teaspoon almond extract
1 ¾   cups flour
2   teaspoons baking powder
¼   teaspoon salt
1   tablespoon milk
½   cup sliced almonds, chopped

In a mixing bowl, cream sugar and butter; beat in egg and extract.
Combine dry ingredients; add to creamed mixture. Divide dough
into fourths; form into 12x3-inch rectangles. Place 5 inches apart
on greased baking sheets. Brush with milk; sprinkle with almonds.
    Bake at 325 degree for 18 to 20 minutes or until firm to the
touch and edges are lightly browned. Cool on baking sheet for
5 minutes before cutting diagonally into 1-inch slices. Remove
to wire racks to cool completely.

ICING

1   cup powdered sugar
¼   teaspoon almond extract
1 to 2 tablespoons milk

Combine icing ingredients; drizzle over bars.

Yields about 4 dozen

Chocolate-Covered Cherry Cookies

1 ½   cups flour
  ½   cup unsweetened cocoa
        dash of salt
  ¼   teaspoon baking powder
  ¼   teaspoon baking soda
  ⅓   cup butter, softened
  1   cup sugar
  1   egg
1 ½   teaspoon vanilla
  1   (10-ounce) jar maraschino cherries

In a large bowl, stir together flour, cocoa, salt, baking powder, and baking soda. In a mixing bowl, cream butter and sugar on low speed until fluffy. Add egg and vanilla; beat well. Stir in dry ingredients and mix well.

   Shape dough into 1-inch balls and place on ungreased cookie sheet. Press down center with thumb.

   Drain cherries; reserving juice. Place half a cherry in the center of each cookie. Bake at 350 degrees for 10 minutes.

Frosting

  1   (6-ounce) package chocolate chips
  ½   cup sweetened condensed milk
  1   tablespoon cherry juice

Combine chocolate chips and milk in a small saucepan and stir over medium heat until chocolate melts. Stir in cherry juice. Spoon 1 teaspoon frosting over each cherry-topped cookie.

Yields 36 cookies

These easy-to-make cookies have a hidden surprise in the center.

103

TIPS ON BAKING COOKIES

* Use glass or plastic cups with spouts for measuring liquids; use metal or plastic nested cups for dry ingredients.

* Lightly spoon flour into measuring cup and level with sharp-edged knife; pack brown sugar firmly into measuring cup.

* Do not use butter or margarine labeled diet, lite, or whipped.

* Use a heavy aluminum cookie sheet.

* To prevent cookies from flattening, chill dough 15 to 30 minutes and use cooled cookie sheet.

* Grease the cookie sheet only if directed, using vegetable shortening or oil spray, not butter or margarine.

* Preheat oven for 10 to 15 minutes and bake only one tray at a time.

* Cool cookies on a wire rack, not on baking tray.

* To keep cookies soft, place a slice of bread in the cookie jar to absorb moisture.

CASHEW COOKIES

8   tablespoons (1 stick) butter or margarine, softened
1   cup firmly packed light brown sugar
1   egg
1   teaspoon vanilla
1   cup sour cream
2   cups all-purpose flour
1   teaspoon baking powder
½   teaspoon baking soda
1   cup unsalted cashews, finely chopped

Cream butter with electric mixer, gradually adding sugar. Blend in egg, vanilla, and sour cream; beat well. In separate bowl, combine flour, baking powder, and soda. Gradually add to creamed mixture, blending after each addition. Stir in cashews.

Drop dough by rounded teaspoonfuls onto lightly greased cookie sheet. Bake at 375 degrees for 8 to 10 minutes or until lightly browned.

FROSTING (optional)

8   tablespoons (1 stick) butter or margarine
2   cups powdered sugar
3   tablespoons cream or milk
     unsalted cashew halves

Heat butter in a saucepan until light amber in color. Remove from heat and add powdered sugar and 3 tablespoons cream or milk. If needed, add more milk to make a smooth creamy icing. Frost each cookie lightly and top with a cashew half.

Yields 3 dozen

COCONUT BREAD

6   eggs, separated
¼   teaspoon cream of tartar
1   cup shortening
8   tablespoons (1 stick) margarine
3   cups sugar
¼   teaspoon salt
1   teaspoon vanilla
1   teaspoon coconut flavoring
3   cups flour
1   cup buttermilk
        with ¼ teaspoon baking soda
1 ½ cups flake coconut

Separate eggs. Beat egg whites with cream of tartar in a small bowl until stiff. In a large bowl, beat egg yolks, shortening, margarine, sugar, salt, vanilla, and coconut flavoring. Add flour and buttermilk-soda mixture alternately. Fold in beaten egg white and add coconut. Pour into 3 greased loaf pans. Bake at 300 degree for 1 hour.

Remove from pans onto waxed paper and sift a light coating of powdered sugar over loaves. Wrap bread in foil and refrigerate for 2 days to improve flavor. Freezes well.

Yields 3 loaves

"At my table, sit with me,
I'll pour coffee or some tea;
Perhaps we'll share our tears
    and laughter;
And be friends for ever after."
~Anonymous

Mary Cassatt's *The Tea*, painted in 1879-1880, features two Victorian ladies and a "tete-a-tete" tea service of three pieces: teapot, sugar bowl, and cream pitcher.

Afternoon tea was introduced around 1840 by Anna, the Duchess of Bedford. Feeling faint in the afternoons, she asked her maid to serve small sandwiches and cakes along with tea. Later she began inviting friends for tea and snacks in the afternoon and a new fashion was born.

The minty green layer makes this perfect for the holidays!

1   cup sugar
1   cup flour
1   (16-ounce) can chocolate syrup
8   tablespoon (1 stick) butter or margarine
4   eggs

8   tablespoons (1 stick) butter or margarine
¼   cup milk
3 ½ cups powdered sugar
2   teaspoons peppermint extract
3   drops green food coloring

1   (6-ounce) package chocolate chips
8   tablespoons (1 stick) butter or margarine

Mix first 5 ingredients and blend thoroughly. Pour into greased 9x13-inch baking dish. Bake at 350 degrees for 20 to 25 minutes. (If using glass dish, cook at 325 degrees.) Cool.

Beat together next 8 tablespoons margarine, milk, powdered sugar, and peppermint until smooth. Add a few drops green food coloring and beat. Spread over cooled brownies and refrigerate at least 30 minutes.

Melt chocolate chips with remaining margarine. Spread over cooled mint layer. Refrigerate or freeze. Cut into squares.

Yields 2 dozen

Mansion chef Jerry Walsh adds the finishing touches to a tray of gingerbread figures with the assistance of Zoë Bednar, and Alex and Andrew Earls.

CRAN-APPLE TARTLETS

1 cup flour
½ cup pecans, finely chopped
¼ cup sugar
4 tablespoons (½ stick) butter, softened
1 egg
1 ½ cups fresh whole cranberries
2 small Granny Smith apples, peeled and diced
1 ½ tablespoons grated orange zest
¾ cup firmly packed brown sugar
½ teaspoon ground cinnamon
   pinch of ground cloves

Combine flour, pecans, and sugar. Blend in butter and egg until mixture begins to crumble. Press dough into bottom and sides of a mini-tart pan or small muffin pan, forming a thin wall. Cover and refrigerate for 1 hour. Preheat oven to 350 degrees. Combine remaining ingredients and spoon into chilled tart shells. Bake for 25 to 30 minutes, or until crust is golden and fruit is bubbly.

Yields 24-30 tarts

A pretty addition to a Christmas tea table.

FEATHERLIGHT CHOCOLATE CHIP COOKIES

2 egg whites
⅔ cup sugar
1 teaspoon vanilla
   pinch of salt

1 (6-ounce) package semisweet chocolate chips
½ cup chopped walnuts

Preheat oven to 350 degrees. Cover a large baking sheet with foil; set aside. In a medium-size bowl, beat egg whites until foamy. Gradually add sugar and beat until stiff peaks form. Mix in vanilla and salt. Fold in chocolate chips and nuts.

Drop by teaspoonfuls 2 inches apart on baking sheet. Put in oven, then turn off heat and leave cookies at least 5 hours without opening door (they can be left overnight). Cookies will be a very light brown in color. Store in airtight container.

Yields 45 cookies

These meringue-based cookies have only 45 calories each.

Holiday Buffet

MOSTACCIOLI PASTA SALAD

1 pound mostaccioli noodles or bow-tie pasta, cooked
½ cup vegetable oil
2 tablespoons mustard
2 teaspoons Worcestershire sauce
¼ cup cider vinegar
½ teaspoon pepper
2 teaspoons garlic
  salt to taste
1 cup green onions, chopped
1 cup cucumber, peeled, seeded, and shredded
1 cup fresh parsley, chopped
½ cup pimentos, diced

Cool and drain noodles. Combine next seven ingredients and add to noodles in large bowl. Add remaining ingredients. Mix well and chill overnight.

Serves 12

HUMMUS WITH PISTACHIO NUTS

1 (16-ounce) can chickpeas, rinsed and drained
⅓ cup tahini (sesame seed paste)
2 cloves garlic, minced and mashed with ½ teaspoon salt
2 tablespoons fresh lemon juice
1 teaspoon cumin
2 tablespoons olive oil
3 tablespoons water
3 tablespoons fresh parsley, minced
  salt and pepper to taste
½ cup pistachio nuts, chopped

In food processor, combine chickpeas, tahini, garlic, lemon juice, cumin, and oil; puree until very smooth. Add water, parsley, salt, and pepper; pulse until blended. Transfer to covered container and refrigerate until ready to serve. Drizzle top with chopped pistachio nuts and serve with pita wedges or baked mini-bagel chips.

Yields 2 cups

(Facing page) The dining room table brims with colorful holiday foods.

Buffet Favorites

Mostaccioli Pasta Salad

Hummus with Pistachio Nuts

Spinach-Cheese Phyllo Triangles

Pimiento Cheese Spread

Mini-Apple Muffins with Honey-Baked Ham

Stuffed Mushrooms

Buffet Ham Loaves with Orange Sauce

Potato Boats

Snow Peas with Herb Cheese

Chicken Satay with Peanut Sauce

Polenta Squares

Fresh Fruit with Yogurt Dip

Holiday Cranberry Punch

South-of-the-Border Salsa

Orange-Nut Mocha Bars

Crudités with Sesame Dip

SPINACH-CHEESE PHYLLO TRIANGLES

These attractive little bundles can be frozen and baked when you need them. Serve on a bed of fresh spinach leaves.

1   (10-ounce) package frozen chopped spinach
⅓   cup minced onion
1   cup plus 3 tablespoons butter or margarine, melted, divided
¼   pound fresh Parmesan cheese, grated
2   eggs, beaten
¾   cup (3 ounces) shredded Monterey Jack or mozzarella cheese
3   tablespoons crumbled blue cheese or feta cheese
2   tablespoons soft bread crumbs
¼   teaspoon salt
¼   teaspoon pepper
¼   teaspoon ground nutmeg
½   (16-ounce) package frozen phyllo pastry, thawed

Thaw spinach; place between paper towels; squeeze out moisture. Sauté onion in 3 tablespoons butter in a large skillet; add spinach and cook 5 minutes. Remove vegetables and cool. Add next 8 ingredients, stirring well. Cut sheets of phyllo lengthwise into 3½-inch strips. Working with one at a time, brush each strip with remaining melted butter. Keep remaining strips covered. Place 2 teaspoons spinach mixture at base of phyllo strip, folding the right bottom corner over into a triangle. Continue folding back and forth into a triangle. Repeat with remaining phyllo. Keep triangles covered before baking. Place triangles, seam side down on ungreased baking sheets. Brush with melted butter; bake at 450 degrees for 10 to 15 minutes.

Yields 3 dozen

PIMIENTO CHEESE SPREAD

Spread on crackers and top with crumbled bacon and finely chopped parsley.

2   cups finely shredded extra sharp cheddar cheese
1   (2-ounce) jar diced pimiento, drained
⅓   cup mayonnaise
⅓   cup chopped pecans, toasted
6   small pimiento-stuffed olives, diced
¼   teaspoon hot sauce
¼   teaspoon black pepper
1   tablespoon dry sherry

Blend together all ingredients and chill.

Yields 2 cups

MINI-APPLE MUFFINS
WITH HONEY-BAKED HAM

2 cups flour
⅔ cup packed light brown sugar
1 tablespoon baking powder
¾ teaspoon ground cinnamon
½ teaspoon salt
1 egg, slightly beaten
⅓ cup butter or margarine, melted
¾ cup milk
¾ cup chunky applesauce
½ cup raisins (optional)
 Dijon-style mustard
¼ pound, honey-baked ham, thinly sliced
 sprigs of watercress, cilantro, or Italian parsley

In a large mixing bowl, stir together flour, brown sugar, baking powder, cinnamon, and salt. Make a well in center and add egg, butter, milk, and applesauce. Stir just until moistened. Fold in raisins, if desired. Fill well-greased 1¾-inch muffin tins almost full. Bake in 400 degree oven about 15 minutes, or until golden brown. Remove from muffin pans and cool completely on a rack. Slice each muffin in half. Spread a thin coat of mustard on cut surfaces. Place one or two thin slices of ham between halves. Insert a sprig of watercress into edges of muffin, allowing leaves to stick out.

Yields 36 muffins

STUFFED MUSHROOMS

12 large mushroom caps
¼ pound prosciutto (Italian ham), julienned
1 teaspoon dried oregano
1 cup mozzarella cheese, grated
1 tablespoon Parmesan cheese, freshly grated
1 teaspoon garlic, minced
1 tablespoon parsley, chopped
 black pepper to taste

Remove mushroom stems and steam caps until slightly crisp. Mix all ingredients by hand, shape into small balls, and stuff into mushroom caps. Top with a little more Parmesan cheese and brown under broiler.

Yields 12

This pleasing combination of apples and ham makes these muffins a great addition to a buffet table.

The taste of garlic, mozzarella cheese, and prosciutto ham enhance this wonderful mushroom appetizer.

BUFFET HAM LOAVES WITH ORANGE SAUCE

These loaves freeze well after baking. Keep on hand for a quick meal or buffet item.

1 pound fresh ground pork
2 pounds ground ham
1 ½ cups bread crumbs
2 eggs
½ to ¾ cup Milnot
½ teaspoon fresh garlic
½ teaspoon pepper
2 tablespoons parsley, finely chopped

Mix first 8 ingredients. Form into loaves or balls. Bake at 350 degrees for 30 minutes. Drain grease, pour on Orange Sauce, and bake another 10 minutes.

Yields 25-30 small loaves

ORANGE SAUCE

1 (6-ounce) can frozen orange juice concentrate, undiluted
½ cup brown sugar
2 tablespoons vinegar

Mix all ingredients together.

The dining room sideboard—a gift from Governor John C. Edwards (1844-1848)—is the oldest piece displayed at the Mansion. It is still used today to serve food during small receptions.

POTATO BOATS

35 tiny (about 1 inch diameter) red potatoes
      olive oil
 8 tablespoons (1 stick) butter, melted
      salt and pepper
 1 cup sour cream
      chives, caviar, cooked crumbled bacon

Preheat oven to 400 degrees. Coat potatoes lightly with oil.
Place on baking sheets and bake until tender, about 30 to 40
minutes. Remove small sliver from one side of each potato and
place cut side down to sit firmly. With a melon ball scoop, create
a small cavity in potatoes. Drizzle with butter and sprinkle with
salt and pepper.   Place a small dollop of sour cream in cavity.
Top with either chives, caviar, or crumbled bacon.

   Note: Small potato slices can also be used for a base. Slice
potato ⅓-inch thick, butter and season as above, and bake for
15 minutes per side, or until golden brown. Top with sour cream
and add toppings.

Yields 35

A thoroughly delicious and attractive addition to any buffet.

SNOW PEAS WITH HERB CHEESE

25 medium-large snow peas
 6 ounces soft cream cheese
 1 teaspoon onion powder (or 3 scallion heads, chopped)
 1 clove garlic, finely chopped
 ¼ cup mixture of chopped fresh basil, dill, and parsley

Blanch peas in boiling water for 45 seconds. Drain and rinse.
Place in bowl of ice water for 1 minute. Dry. Dry on a paper
towel. Combine remaining ingredients in a bowl, mixing well.

   Using a sharp knife, split the snow peas on curved side.
Using a pastry bag, fill each pea pod with the cream cheese
mixture.

   Note: Make a pastry bag by snipping a small corner from a
heavy plastic freezer bag.

Yields 25

Create a lively buffet table by offering foods in a variety of colors and shapes, such as these stuffed snow peas.

CHICKEN SATAY WITH PEANUT SAUCE

This is a reduced fat version of a buffet favorite. For Beef Satay, use 1½ pounds lean boneless beef strips in place of chicken.

6 boneless skinless chicken breasts
2 tablespoons fresh lime juice
1 tablespoon soy sauce
1 teaspoon vegetable oil
2 cloves garlic, minced
½ teaspoon paprika
⅛ teaspoon cayenne
   bamboo skewers

Pound chicken breasts into ¼-inch thickness. Cut each into ½-inch by 3-inch-long strips. Combine remaining ingredients and add chicken strips. Marinate in a shallow non-metallic dish at least 2 hours, or overnight, in refrigerator.

Remove chicken from marinade and thread accordion-style onto bamboo skewers that have been soaked in water for 30 minutes. Arrange skewers on baking sheets. Bake at 350 degrees for 8 to 10 minutes, or until cooked through (if using a grill, cook for 10 to 12 minutes). Serve chicken hot with Peanut Sauce at room temperature.

Yields 50 pieces

PEANUT SAUCE

3 tablespoons creamy peanut butter
1 teaspoon sesame oil
1 tablespoon soy sauce
2 teaspoons sugar
¾ tablespoon lemon juice
1 garlic clove, minced
   dash cayenne pepper
¾ cup hot water

Combine all the ingredients except water in a medium saucepan and simmer for about 2 to 6 minutes, or until blended. Place sauce in a food processor and slowly add water, blending to make a smooth sauce.

Yields 1 ½ cups

POLENTA SQUARES

12 tablespoons yellow cornmeal
3 cups canned low-salt chicken broth
2 garlic cloves
1 teaspoon salt
dash of pepper
½ cup fresh grated Parmesan cheese
1 (7-ounce) can whole green chilies, drained
1 cup corn, drained
⅔ cup chopped sun-dried tomatoes
2 cups grated Monterey Jack cheese

Preheat oven to 400 degrees. Butter or spray a 9x13-inch baking dish. Mix cornmeal, broth, and garlic in medium saucepan. Bring to a boil over medium heat, whisking constantly. Reduce to a moderately low heat. Cook until polenta is very thick, stirring often, about 12 to 15 minutes. Season with salt and pepper; stir in Parmesan cheese. Pour polenta into prepared dish and smooth top. Cover with chilies and corn. Sprinkle with sun-dried tomatoes and cheese.

Bake until polenta puffs and cheese begins to brown, about 25 minutes. Let sit for a few minutes before cutting into squares.

Yields 16 squares

A real crowd pleaser!

FRESH FRUIT WITH YOGURT DIP

2 cups vanilla yogurt
½ cup honey or low-sugar orange marmalade
1 teaspoon ground cinnamon
assorted fresh fruit (apples, bananas, pineapple, strawberries, pears, grapes, melon)

Combine yogurt, honey, and cinnamon in a small bowl; stir to blend. Place bowl on platter. Surround with fruit cut into bite-size pieces.

Yields about 2 cups

Fruit is a welcomed addition to any buffet table, especially among your calorie conscious guests.

HOLIDAY CRANBERRY PUNCH

Here's proof that a good punch doesn't have to be complicated or sugary.

4 cups cranberry juice cocktail, chilled
2 cups orange juice, chilled
12-ounce sugar free (or regular) lemon-lime soda, chilled

Combine cranberry and orange juices in a punch bowl with an ice ring. Pour the carbonated beverage down the sides of the bowl.

Serves 18

SOUTH-OF-THE-BORDER SALSA

Make your own fresh tomato salsa with this quick and tasty recipe.

6 cups coarsely chopped, peeled ripe tomatoes
1 (7½-ounce) can tomato sauce
½ teaspoon salt
4 fresh jalapeno peppers, seeded and chopped (or small can diced green chilies, drained)
6 garlic cloves, crushed, about 2 tablespoons
1 tablespoon paprika
1 tablespoon ground cumin
2 onions, finely chopped
½ cup fresh coriander, finely chopped, divided
3 tablespoons fresh lime juice

Combined tomatoes in a medium-sized saucepan with tomato sauce; add salt, peppers, garlic, paprika, and cumin. Bring to a boil over high heat, stirring often. Reduce heat to medium-low and boil gently, uncovered, stirring often for 10 minutes.

Stir onions and ¼ cup chopped coriander into salsa. Continue cooking, stirring often, until most of liquid has evaporated, about 5 to 10 minutes.

Remove salsa from heat and stir in remaining ¼ cup coriander and lime juice. Taste and add more lime juice, if desired. Refrigerate in a sealed jar. Salsa will keep for a week or can be frozen.

Serve with tortilla chips or your favorite Mexican dish.

Yields 7 cups

Orange-Nut Mocha Bars

1 cup (2 sticks) unsalted butter
4 ounces unsweetened chocolate
4 ounces semisweet or bittersweet chocolate
2 cups sugar
5 eggs
1 ½ cups flour
2 tablespoons Grand Marnier
1 tablespoon coffee extract (or 2 teaspoons instant coffee powder)
1 tablespoon grated orange zest
  dash of salt
1 cup pecans, chopped

Melt the butter and chocolates in double boiler or in microwave.
Cream sugar and eggs; stir into cooled chocolate. Stir in remaining
ingredients and blend well. Spoon batter into a greased and floured
9x13-inch baking pan and bake at 350 degrees for 20 to 25 minutes.
Bars will be moist when cake tester is inserted. Let cool in pan for
30 minutes and refrigerate before cutting into squares.

Yields 24-30 bars

A wonderful brownie with a hint of citrus and mocha.

Crudités with Sesame Dip

½ cup light mayonnaise
¼ cup light sour cream
2 tablespoons soy sauce
2 tablespoons chopped fresh basil
1 tablespoon sesame oil
1 tablespoon toasted sesame seeds
1 tablespoon rice vinegar
1 teaspoon fresh ginger, peeled and minced
1 teaspoon sugar
½ teaspoon dry mustard
⅛ teaspoon cayenne pepper
  salt and pepper

Combine all ingredient in small bowl; whisk to blend. Season dip
with salt and pepper to taste; refrigerate. Serve with raw or slightly
blanched vegetables.

Yields 1 cup

Heaping platters of colorful, cut-up vegetables—often referred to as crudités (kroo-dee-TAYS)—provide your guests with healthy, attractive party foods.

Family Holiday Dinner

A Christmas family party!
We know nothing in nature more delightful!
There seems a magic in the very name of Christmas.
~Charles Dickens "Sketches by Boz"

ORANGE-GLAZED SWEET POTATOES

4   medium sweet potatoes
¼   teaspoon salt
1   cup orange juice
¼   cup raisins
½   cup brown sugar
1   tablespoon cornstarch, dissolved in small amount of water
4   tablespoons (½ stick) butter or margarine
3   tablespoons sherry
2   tablespoons walnuts, chopped
½   teaspoon orange peel, grated

Cook potatoes in boiling salted water until tender; drain, peel, and halve lengthwise (or use 3 cups canned sweet potatoes). Arrange in shallow baking dish. Sprinkle lightly with salt. In saucepan, combine orange juice, raisins, and brown sugar; bring quickly to a boil. Add remaining ingredients; pour over potatoes. Bake uncovered at 350 degrees for 20 minutes, or until potatoes are well glazed.

Serves 6

GERMAN RED CABBAGE

8   tablespoons (1 stick) butter or margarine
1   medium head red cabbage, shredded
3   tart apples, diced
3   tablespoons lemon juice
3   teaspoons brown sugar
    salt to taste

Melt butter in large skillet. Add all other ingredients and cover. Simmer for 45 to 50 minutes or until cabbage is tender.

Serves 6-8

(Facing page) A Victorian family celebrates the holiday season as portrayed in this 19th-century drawing from *Harper's Weekly*.

Holiday Dinner Side Dishes

Orange-Glazed Sweet Potatoes

German Red Cabbage

Roasted Mediterranean Vegetables

Cranberry-Apple Frappé

Squash Stir Fry

Old-Fashioned Applesauce

Brussels Sprouts au Gratin

Spoon Bread

Cranberry Sauce with Dried Cherries

Corn Relish

Cornbread Stuffing with Toasted Pecans

Ozark Bread Pudding with Rum Sauce

Apricot Brandy Pound Cake

Spinach Cashew Salad with Poppy Seed Dressing

Swiss Green Beans

Holiday Rice Casserole

A VICTORIAN CHRISTMAS DINNER:
A BOUNTIFUL FEAST

Christmas Day during the late 19th century was a bountiful, day-long feast. Food appeared on the table early with a breakfast of oatmeal or pearl hominy. Even French chops, peas, creamed potatoes, and hot rolls were offered the early riser, along with an assortment of fruits.

Lunch came around one o'clock with the arrival of more food from the kitchen: bouillon, thin slices of roast beef, ham or tongue, hash browns, sardines with sliced lemon, and more fruit. All was washed down with hearty amounts of coffee, hot chocolate, or tea.

While awaiting the evening meal, family members often took a walk or a nap. Meanwhile, the lady of the house trotted out her best table linen and dinnerware for the final meal of the day.

The First Lady of the Mansion likely followed the same custom. If she was fortunate enough to have a full complement of silver and china, she could fashion an elegant holiday table for family and guests. But all too often she had to make do with mismatched, hand-me-downs from previous administrations.

While the First Lady saw to the table arrangements, Mansion servants prepared the meal in the basement kitchen. Food was delivered to the dining room by way of a dumbwaiter located in the first-floor butler's pantry. Servers—most often prison inmates—worked swiftly to deliver the food to the table at its intended temperature.

The evening feast customarily began with a consommé, followed by such delicacies as terrapin stew, roast turkey, oyster dressing, country ham, and cranberry jelly.

Often a lettuce salad with French dressing was served after the meat course along with cheese and biscuits. The highly regarded Christmas pudding, calling for a pound of kidney suet and a cooking time of over four hours, topped off the meal, ending a full day of eating, visiting, and celebration.

ROASTED MEDITERRANEAN VEGETABLES

8   medium carrots, bias-sliced 1-inch thick (about 4 cups)
3   small potatoes, quartered (about 2 cups)
2   small zucchini, sliced and halved
2   small yellow squash, sliced and halved
1   red pepper, cut in ¾-inch pieces
1   green pepper, cut in ¾-inch pieces
1   red onion, cut in chunks
    garlic salt
    pepper to taste
2   teaspoons Italian seasoning
2   cloves garlic, minced
4   tablespoons olive oil
2   tablespoons fresh parsley

In a large covered saucepan, parboil carrots and potatoes in small amount of boiling water for 6 minutes; drain. Spread partially cooked vegetables evenly on a metal cookie sheet. Add other uncooked vegetables. Sprinkle with garlic salt, pepper, and Italian seasoning. Combine garlic and olive oil; drizzle and toss gently. Bake for 30 minutes at 425 degrees, or until tender, stirring once. Sprinkle with parsley.

Serves 8-10

Packed with nutrition and flavor.

CRANBERRY-APPLE FRAPPÉ

1   cup chilled cranberry juice cocktail
1   cup chilled apple juice
1   small ripe banana, peeled, cut into chunks
¼   cup sugar
2   tablespoons chilled milk
1   teaspoon fresh lemon juice
4-6 ice cubes

Combine all ingredients, except ice cubes, in a blender and process until smooth. Add ice cubes and process until frothy. Pour into glasses.

Serves 3-4

Serve this delightful fruit frappé at breakfast on Christmas morning. Refreshing and smooth anytime.

SQUASH STIR FRY

You can vary the amount of squash and cheese depending on what you have on hand. This becomes an execellent one-dish meal with the addition of cooked ground beef.

2 tablespoons olive oil or vegetable oil
2 garlic cloves, minced
1 large onion, sliced and separated into rings
3 medium-size zucchini, thinly sliced
3 medium-size yellow squash, thinly sliced
1 tomato, diced, or ½ cup spaghetti sauce
¾ teaspoon salt
½ teaspoon pepper
½ cup shredded cheddar cheese (not low-fat cheese)
¼ cup Parmesan cheese, or to taste

Pour oil in large skillet. Sauté garlic, onion, and squash until well done, about 10 minutes. Add tomato or sauce, salt, and pepper. Add cheeses and cook until melted.

Serves 6

OLD-FASHIONED APPLESAUCE

A simple dish from our childhood can still be a family delight.

6 pounds apples, quartered and cored (use Fuji, Braeburn, Jonathan, or Granny Smith apples)
½ cup apple juice or water
¼ cup sugar
1 teaspoon ground cinnamon
¼ teaspoon ground nutmeg

Combine all ingredients in heavy 3-quart saucepan. Cover and cook over medium-low heat until apples are tender, stirring occasionally, about 45 minutes. Pour juice and all into a food mill and process (the mill separates the skins). Put applesauce in bowl and add sugar and spices.

Note: Add a handful of red-hot cinnamon candies to warm applesauce if more color and zing are desired.

Yields 1½ quarts

Brussels Sprouts au Gratin

BRUSSELS SPROUTS AU GRATIN

¼ cup fine dry breadcrumbs
1 tablespoon grated Parmesan cheese
2 pounds fresh Brussels sprouts or 2 (10-ounce)
    packages frozen
2 tablespoons (¼ stick) butter or margarine
2 tablespoons flour
1 ½ cups milk
1 cup shredded Gruyere or Swiss cheese
1 tablespoon white wine Worcestershire sauce
½ teaspoon salt
¼ teaspoon pepper
¼ teaspoon paprika

Combine breadcrumbs and Parmesan cheese; set aside. Trim ends from Brussels sprouts and cut in half lengthwise. Cook fresh sprouts in boiling water for 12 minutes, or until barely tender. (Cook frozen sprouts according to package directions.) Drain and place in lightly greased 1½-quart baking dish. Set aside.

Melt butter in saucepan over low heat; blend in flour, stirring until smooth. Cook, stirring constantly for 1 minute. Gradually add milk; cook over medium heat, stirring constantly until thick.

Add cheese and next 3 ingredients, stirring until cheese melts. Spoon sauce over Brussels sprouts; top with breadcrumb mixture and sprinkle with paprika. Bake uncovered at 350 degrees for 20 minutes, or until brown and bubbly.

Serves 8

SPOON BREAD

1 ½ cups water
2 cups milk
1 ½ cups cornmeal, sifted
1 ¼ teaspoons salt
1 ½ teaspoons sugar
2 tablespoons (¼ stick) butter
5 eggs, separated
1 tablespoon baking powder

When I was growing up, there was never a holiday meal without this Southern favorite.

Preheat oven to 375 degrees. Combine water and milk in saucepan and heat to simmer. Add cornmeal, salt, sugar, and butter. Stir constantly over medium heat until thickened to consistency of mush, about 5 minutes.

Remove and cool slightly. Beat egg yolks and add to mixture. Beat whites until stiff and peaks form. Gently fold into mixture along with baking powder just before cooking.

Pour into buttered 2-quart casserole or soufflé dish. Bake uncovered at 375 degrees for 45 minutes or until puffed and golden brown. Serve immediately. (Note: Insert cake tester in middle to check doneness. Center will drop some as bread cools.)

Serves 8

This Christmas 1903 menu from the City Hotel in St. Louis lists dishes that were also served at the Mansion at the turn of the century.

CRANBERRY SAUCE WITH DRIED CHERRIES

2 ½ cups cranberry juice cocktail
1 (8-ounce) package dried tart cherries, about 2 cups
1 cup sugar
1 (12-ounce) package fresh cranberries
¼ teaspoon ground cloves

Bring juice to simmer in heavy saucepan. Remove from heat and add cherries. Let stand 8 minutes. Mix in sugar, then cranberries and cloves. Cook over medium heat until cranberries burst, stirring occasionally, about 10 minutes. Refrigerate until cold, about 4 hours. Sauce will thicken as it cools. Can be prepared a day ahead.

Yields 4½ cups

Cranberries and cherries go well together in this traditional holiday sauce.

CORN RELISH

2 (16-ounce) packages frozen corn, thawed
3 small zucchinis, diced ¼-inch
1 (16-ounce) can tomatoes, drained and diced ¼-inch
1 medium onion, diced ¼-inch
⅔ cup olive oil
4 tablespoons fresh lime juice
2 tablespoons white wine vinegar
1 teaspoons celery seed
1 teaspoon mustard seed
1 ½ teaspoons salt
½ teaspoon garlic salt
1 teaspoon pepper

Combine vegetables in a large bowl. In a jar with a tight lid, combine oil with remaining ingredients; shake well. Pour over vegetables and stir gently. Chill several hours or overnight. Serve with poultry or ham.

Yields 8-10 servings

Make this relish a day ahead to allow the flavors to blend.

CORNBREAD STUFFING WITH TOASTED PECANS

Each family has its favorite dressing—this is ours.

1   pound medium-flavored bulk sausage
1   cup (2 sticks) butter or margarine
1   medium onion, finely chopped
1   cup celery, finely chopped
1   cup toasted pecans, chopped (optional)
2-3 eggs
2   small packages cornbread dressing (or part dry Italian bread or biscuits)
1-2 cans chicken-rice soup
1   teaspoon poultry seasoning
    pepper to taste

Crumble and brown sausage in large skillet; drain and transfer to large bowl. Add butter or margarine to pan and sauté onions and celery. Combine vegetables with sausage in large bowl along with pecans, eggs, and dressing or bread. Add enough soup to moisten. Add seasonings to taste. Stuff turkey loosely with mixture. Spoon remainder lightly into a greased 9-inch baking dish and bake uncovered at 350 degrees for 30 minutes.

Serves 8-10

OZARK BREAD PUDDING WITH RUM SAUCE

This homey American classic is always a welcomed dessert.

5-6 baked biscuits, crumbled
2   cups milk
4   eggs, well beaten
¾   cup sugar
4   tablespoons (½ stick) butter or margarine, melted
1   teaspoon vanilla extract
¼   cup raisins (optional)

Combine all ingredients; stir well. Pour into a 1½-quart casserole. Pour ½ inch water into a baking dish and place casserole into dish. Bake at 350 degrees for 1 hour or until knife inserted in center comes out clean.

RUM SAUCE

Combine ½ cup sugar, ¼ cup water, 2 tablespoons butter or margarine in a small saucepan. Bring to a boil for 1 minute, or until sugar is dissolved. Remove from heat and stir in 1 tablespoon of rum. Serve warm over bread pudding.

Serves 6-8

APRICOT BRANDY POUND CAKE

1 cup (2 sticks) butter, softened
3 cups sugar
6 eggs
3 cups flour
¼ teaspoon baking soda
½ teaspoon salt
1 (8-ounce) carton sour cream
½ cup apricot brandy
1 teaspoon rum extract
1 teaspoon vanilla
1 teaspoon orange extract

A lovely holiday dessert served with fresh fruit. This cake is even better a few days after baking.

Beat butter on medium speed with an electric mixer for 2 minutes, or until creamy. Gradually add sugar, beating until light and fluffy. Add eggs, one at a time, beating just until yellow disappears.

Combine flour, baking soda, and salt in medium mixing bowl; stir well. Add flour mixture to batter; stirring just until blended. Add sour cream, brandy, and flavorings; stir well. Pour batter into a greased, floured, and waxed paper-lined 10-inch tube pan.

Bake at 325 degrees for 1 hour and 15 minutes, or until cake tests done. Cool in pan on wire rack for 10 minutes; remove and cool completely on wire rack.

Yields one 10-inch cake

The Missouri Children's Fountain on the Mansion lawn is the work of Missouri sculptor Jamie Anderson. The figure atop the fountain portrays the daughter of Governor and Mrs. T. T. Crittenden. The nine-year-old youngster died of diphtheria just five days before Christmas 1882.

SPINACH CASHEW SALAD
WITH POPPY SEED DRESSING

½ pound bacon, chopped
5 ounces spinach
½ head lettuce, about 8 ounces
½ cup cashew nuts, pieces
½ cup mozzarella cheese, grated

Truly a special occasion salad.

Fry bacon until crisp. Drain on paper towel; set aside. Wash spinach and lettuce and tear into bite-size pieces. Place in salad bowl. Add cashew pieces, grated cheese, and crumbled bacon. Toss and serve with poppy seed dressing.

Serves 8-12

POPPY SEED DRESSING

⅔ cup oil
⅓ cup sugar
⅓ cup red wine vinegar

¼ teaspoon dry mustard
1 ½ teaspoons red onion, finely grated
1 tablespoon poppy seeds

Place all ingredients in blender and process until smooth. Dress salad just before serving.

Yields 1½ cups

SWISS GREEN BEANS

3 (16-ounce) cans cut green beans, drained
½ cup onion, chopped
1 tablespoon butter
2 tablespoons flour
1 cup milk
½ to ¾ cup Swiss cheese, grated
½ cup sour cream
1 tablespoon sugar
½ teaspoon salt
2 cups stuffing mix, or buttered bread crumbs

My mother-in-law gave me this recipe many years ago and I have served it at every holiday meal since.

Place green beans in a 13x9-inch glass pan. In a large frying pan, sauté onions in butter. Add flour, stir. Gradually add milk; bring to a boil. Add cheese, sour cream, sugar, and salt. Cook until thick and cheese is melted. Pour mixture over green beans. Top with stuffing mix or buttered bread crumbs. Bake at 350 degrees for 25 to 30 minutes.

Serves 8-10

HOLIDAY RICE CASSEROLE

4 tablespoons (½ stick) margarine, melted
1 medium onion, chopped
1 cup white rice, uncooked
2 (4-ounce) cans mushrooms, undrained
1 can onion soup, plus 1 can water

2 teaspoons low-salt soy sauce
1 teaspoon Worcestershire sauce
2 cloves garlic, minced
1½ tablespoons brown gravy sauce
pepper to taste
1 can sliced water chestnuts (optional)

Sauté onion in margarine. Add rice and brown lightly. Combine with remaining ingredients. Place in 13x9x2-inch baking dish. Bake uncovered at 350 degrees for 25 minutes. Add water chestnuts, if desired, for extra crunch.

Christmas Day 1886—a typical family gathering as
portrayed in *Humphrey's Magazine*, a St. Louis publication.

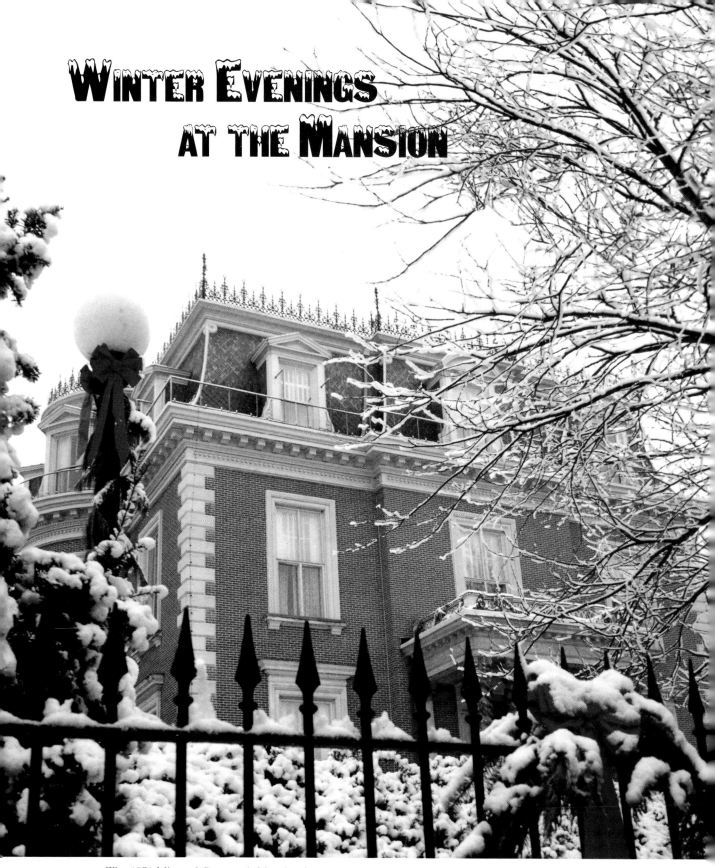

WINTER EVENINGS AT THE MANSION

The 1871 Missouri Governor's Mansion framed by snow-covered evergreens and trees draped with icicles.

CHICKEN MARSALA

2 eggs, slightly beaten
¾ cup milk
4 chicken breast halves, boned and skinned
2 cups Italian bread crumbs, fine
4 tablespoons (½ stick) butter
4 ounces fresh mushrooms, sliced
1 cup Marsala wine
   salt and pepper to taste

Mix eggs and milk. Place bread crumbs in shallow pan. Trim fat from chicken. Dip chicken pieces in egg mixture then into bread crumbs. Melt butter in a skillet; add chicken and brown on both sides. Add mushrooms, wine, salt, and pepper; cover, reduce heat, and simmer 30 minutes.

Serves 4

NUT-ENCRUSTED TROUT

¼ cup pecans
¼ cup pine nuts
1 tablespoon sesame seeds
4 trout, boned
4 tablespoons (½ stick) butter
1 large garlic clove, minced
   salt and pepper
2 tablespoons oil, divided, for skillet

Finely chop nuts in processor using on/off turns. Transfer to shallow bowl and mix in sesame seeds. Open trout; place skin side down on a large baking sheet. Stir butter and garlic in small saucepan over low heat until butter melts. Brush garlic butter over trout. Season with salt and pepper. Sprinkle nut mixture over trout, pressing to adhere. Chill uncovered for 30 minutes. Heat 1 tablespoon oil in large non-stick skillet over medium-high heat. Place 2 trout, nut side down, into skillet. Cook 2 minutes. Using spatula, turn trout, nut side up, onto baking sheet. Repeat with remaining oil and trout. Bake trout until opaque in center, about 5 minutes.

Serves 4

Food for Winter Evenings
at Home

Chicken Marsala

Nut-Encrusted Trout

Tarragon Lamb

Chicken Chalupas

Oriental Chicken Salad
with Soy-Ginger
Vinaigrette

Chicken Noodle Soup

Baja Chicken

Spaghetti Meat Sauce

Farfalle Carbonara

Ozark Grilled Catfish

Beef Brisket

Minestrone Soup
with Pasta and Greens

Eggplant Parmigiana

Pasta Primavera
with Basil Sauce

TARRAGON LAMB

1   tablespoon olive oil
4   tablespoons (½ stick) butter, divided
8   boneless lamb chops, cut 1-inch thick
      salt and pepper to taste
¼   cup brandy
3   tablespoons whipping cream
2   tablespoons chopped fresh tarragon

Heat oil and half the butter in a heavy skillet. Add lamb and cook several minutes on each side until well browned, but still slightly pink in the center. Transfer to serving plate; season with salt and pepper.

   Add remaining butter to pan. When melted, add brandy and bring to a boil. Stir in cream and tarragon; cook until thick. Season with salt and pepper; pour over lamb. Garnish with fresh tarragon or parsley.

Yields 4 servings

CHICKEN CHALUPAS

¾   pound cheddar cheese, grated, divided
¾   cup Monterey Jack cheese, grated, divided
1   can chicken soup
½   cup chopped green onions with tops
1   small onion, chopped
1   pint sour cream
1   small can green chilies
4   large chicken breasts, cooked and diced
10-12 medium flour tortillas

Set aside ½ of the cheddar and Jack cheeses. Combine all remaining ingredients, except chicken and tortillas. Set aside 1 ½ cups of this mixture. Add chicken to remainder.

   Place 3 tablespoons chicken mixture on each tortilla. Roll up and place seam side down in 9x9-inch casserole. Top with remaining mixture and rest of cheeses.

   Refrigerate overnight. Bake for 45 minutes in a 350 degree oven.

Serves 6

ORIENTAL CHICKEN SALAD
WITH SOY-GINGER VINAIGRETTE

4   chicken breast halves
½   cup teriyaki sauce
4   cups iceberg lettuce, thinly shredded
2   cups green cabbage, thinly shredded
2   large carrots, grated

A one-dish meal that you can make ahead and assemble just before serving.

Brush chicken with teriyaki sauce. Line baking sheet with foil and cook chicken in 375 degree oven, about 15 minutes. Cool completely. Cut cooked chicken into strips and set aside. Combine lettuce, cabbage, carrots, and chicken strips. Toss with Soy-Ginger Vinaigrette and top with garnish.

Yields 2 ½ cups

SOY-GINGER VINAIGRETTE

¼   cup soy sauce
2   tablespoons rice wine vinegar
2   tablespoons vegetable oil
2   tablespoons dark sesame oil
2   tablespoons sugar
2   tablespoons hoisin sauce

⅓   cup water
½   teaspoon chili garlic sauce
1   teaspoon minced fresh ginger
⅓   cup smooth peanut butter
¼   teaspoon minced mint leaves
½   teaspoon minced fresh cilantro

Combine soy sauce, vinegar, oils, sugar, hoisin sauce, water, chili garlic sauce, and ginger. Mix well. Put peanut butter into a food blender and combine with liquid. Process until smooth; remove to a bowl. Stir in mint and cilantro. Use only enough of the sauce to lightly dress the salad.

Yields 1 cup

GARNISH

12   wonton sheets, cut into ¼-inch strips and fried in ½ cup oil
        until crisp and golden, about 45 seconds
2   teaspoons sesame seeds
¼   cup roasted peanuts

CHICKEN NOODLE SOUP

A hearty soup for a cold winter night.

8 cups boiling water
1 large whole chicken
2 medium onions, diced
2 cups celery, chopped
2 green peppers, diced
10 medium carrots (about 2 cups), diced
1 (8-ounce) can mushrooms, drained
½ teaspoon garlic salt
1 teaspoon black pepper
½ teaspoon curry powder
2 bay leaves
1 teaspoon Beau Monde seasoning
1 tablespoon Italian seasoning
2 tablespoons chicken flavored bouillon granules
1 teaspoon poultry seasoning
1 tablespoon salt
1 (26-ounce) package frozen egg noodles, not dry noodles

Place all ingredients, except noodles, in boiling water; cook over medium heat for 1 hour, or until chicken separates from bone. Allow mixture to cool. Remove chicken, debone, and shred. Skim grease from top of soup (or refrigerate until grease solidifies). Return meat to stock; bring to a boil. Add noodles and cook until tender, according to package directions.

Serves 8

BAJA CHICKEN

Looking for a quick, nutrious dish? This tarragon and sherry flavored chicken is the answer.

8 chicken breast halves, boned
   seasoned salt and pepper to taste
2 cloves garlic, crushed
4 tablespoons olive oil
4 tablespoons tarragon vinegar
⅔ cup dry sherry wine

Sprinkle chicken with seasonings. Crush garlic into oil and vinegar in a skillet. Sauté chicken until golden brown. Remove to baking dish. Pour sherry over pieces and cook at 350 degree for 10 minutes.

Serves 8

SPAGHETTI MEAT SAUCE

¼ cup oil
2 medium onions
2 cloves garlic, minced
2 pounds ground beef
3 (15-ounce) cans tomatoes (7 cups), undrained
2 (6-ounce) cans tomato paste
3 bay leaves
½ cup celery
¼ cup fresh parsley, chopped
1 tablespoon salt
2 tablespoons sugar
¼ teaspoon basil
¼ teaspoon black pepper
1 teaspoon oregano (optional)
½ cup water, if needed

Heat oil in large pot. Add onions and garlic; sauté 5 minutes. Add ground beef; cook until brown, breaking up meat with a fork as it cooks. Stir in remaining ingredients, except water which is used only if sauce becomes too thick. Smash tomatoes with your hand as they are added.

Bring to a simmer and cook over low heat until thick, about 45 to 60 minutes. Do not overcook. Remove bay leaves and skim off any excess fat. Serve over cooked spaghetti noodles. Freezes well.

Serves 6

This is an old favorite originally published in the Bible Cookbook *many years ago.*

Popular sale items at the Governor's Mansion are the pewter ornaments of the Mansion and the USS *Missouri* punch bowl.

FARFALLE CARBONARA

Prosciutto ham and farfalle (pronounced: fahr-FAH-lay) team up in this Italian classic. But cooked tortellini also works well in place of the bow-tie pasta.

2 tablespoons (¼ stick) butter
3 garlic cloves, finely chopped
6 ounces prosciutto ham, cut into thin strips
2 cups light cream
1 ½ teaspoons chicken bouillon granules
⅓ cup dry white wine
⅓ cup Parmesan cheese, freshly grated
   salt and pepper to taste
2 tablespoons cornstarch, dissolved in small amount of water
1 cup small frozen peas
1 pound farfalle (bow-tie) pasta, cooked according to directions

Melt butter in a saucepan; add garlic and prosciutto ham. Sauté until soft but not brown. Add cream and bring to a slow simmer. Add chicken bouillon granules, wine, and cheese. Return to a slow simmer. Add salt and pepper to taste. Add cornstarch-water mixture a little at a time, until sauce is slightly thick. Add peas and combine with cooked farfalle pasta.

Serves 4

OZARK GRILLED CATFISH

Missouri's many streams and rivers offer an abundance of fresh water fish.

4 whole catfish
½ cup soy sauce
½ cup sherry wine
2-3 garlic cloves, chopped
2 tablespoons vegetable oil
1 lemon, squeezed
   wood chips for grill

Combine all ingredients and marinate fish 30 minutes. Turn fish and marinate another 30 minutes. Soak wood chips in water 30 minutes; drain. Divide hot coals. Push half to each side and place soaked chips on top coals. Place fish in rack on grill, but not directly over the coals. Cover grill and cook 45 to 60 minutes, depending on size of fish. Do not turn fish. Fish will be smokey-flavored and golden when done.

Serves 4

BEEF BRISKET

3	tablespoons vegetable oil, divided
5-6	pound beef brisket, seasoned with salt and pepper
3	large yellow onions, cut into ½-inch pieces, about 5 cups
1-3	large garlic cloves, minced
1	teaspoon paprika
¾	teaspoon salt
¾	teaspoon freshly ground pepper
3	cups water

Preheat oven to 375 degrees. In a Dutch oven or other heavy baking pan, heat 1 tablespoon of oil for 10 minutes. Pat brisket dry and season with salt and pepper. Roast brisket in pan, uncovered, 30 minutes.

In a large skillet, cook onions in remaining 2 tablespoons oil over moderately high heat, stirring until softened. Reduce heat and continue cooking until onions are deep golden in color. Stir in garlic, paprika, salt, and pepper; cook 1 minute. Stir in water and bring to boil.

Spoon onion mixture over brisket and bake with lid ½-inch ajar for 3 to 4 hours, or until brisket is tender. Check pan occasionally and add more water, if needed.

Remove brisket from oven and let cool in onion mixture 1 hour. Remove brisket from pan, scraping onion mixture back into pan; wrap in foil and chill overnight. Spoon onion mixture into a 1-quart container; cover and chill overnight.

Discard fat from onion mixture, add enough water to mixture to measure 3 cups total, and mix in a blender until smooth.

Trim fat from brisket and slice thinly against the grain. Warm gravy in skillet, add brisket, and heat in oven 30 minutes.

Note: If a barbecued brisket is desired instead of gravy, add your favorite sauce to sliced meat and rewarm.

Serves 8-10

The long, slow cooking makes this an extremely tender and tasty dish.

MINESTRONE SOUP WITH PASTA AND GREENS

Serve with crusty
Italian bread for a
great one-dish meal.

¼ cup yellow onion, finely chopped
2 tablespoons (¼ stick) butter
1 tablespoon olive oil
2 tablespoons pancetta (Italian bacon), finely diced
¼ cup carrots, peeled and finely diced
¼ cup celery, finely diced
¼ teaspoon dried rosemary
1 ½ cups Swiss chard or spinach leaves, roughly chopped
1 cup mustard green leaves or kale, roughly chopped
1 ½ cups butter lettuce leaves, roughly chopped
2 cups savory cabbage leaves, finely shredded
salt and pepper to taste
1 beef bouillon cube dissolved in 5 cups water
6 ounces cavatappi noodles or small macaroni noodles
¼ cup Parmigiano-Reggiano cheese, freshly grated

In a heavy stockpot, sauté onion in butter and oil. Stir in the pancetta; cook until lightly brown, but not crisp. Add carrots, celery, and rosemary; sauté until lightly browned. Drop in all the greens; season with salt and pepper. When greens wilt, add bouillon mixture and bring to boil. Reduce heat, cover, and cook for 1 hour. Return soup to boil; drop in pasta. Cover; cook until pasta is done. Pour soup in bowl; sprinkle with cheese.

Serves 8

EGGPLANT PARMIGIANA

This quick, lighter version
of an old favorite is perfect
for an evening meal.

1 eggplant, peeled, thinly sliced
¼ cup olive oil
salt to taste
1 cup prepared spaghetti sauce
1 tablespoon fresh basil, chopped
½ cup Parmesan cheese, freshly grated

Sauté eggplant in olive oil until brown. Drain and salt. Place eggplant in an oiled casserole dish. Top eggplant with sauce and basil. Sprinkle with cheese and bake for 10 to 15 minutes. Serve warm.

Serves 4

PASTA PRIMAVERA with Basil Sauce

1 tablespoon vegetable oil
¾ pound uncooked fettuccine
1 bunch broccoli separated into flowerets
2 medium zucchini, cut into ¼-inch slices
1 bunch scallions, thinly sliced

1 sweet red pepper, cut into 1-inch slices
1 (6-ounce) can black olives, drained and sliced
2 cups cubed cooked chicken breasts
⅔ cup freshly grated Parmesan cheese, divided
    salt and freshly ground pepper to taste

Add oil to 3 quarts boiling salted water. Cook pasta, rinse with cold water, and drain. Combine vegetables and chicken with pasta. Fold in ⅔ of the Basil Sauce and ⅓ cup cheese. Season with salt and pepper. (Dish may now be refrigerated overnight.) To serve, add remaining sauce, taste and adjust seasonings; sprinkle with remaining cheese.

Serves 8

BASIL SAUCE

¼ cup minced fresh basil
1 garlic clove
2 eggs
½ teaspoon dry mustard
1 tablespoon tarragon vinegar

½ teaspoon lemon juice
½ teaspoon salt
1 ½ cups vegetable oil
½ cup sour cream

Mince basil and garlic in a food processor. Add eggs, mustard, vinegar, lemon juice, and salt; mix well. With machine running, add oil in a thin, slow stream until blended. Use only enough oil to produce a medium-thick mayonnaise. Add sour cream, process several minutes. Refrigerate until ready to use.

Note: This recipe from Mansion cookbook *Past & Repast* is reprinted by popular demand.

Governor and Mrs. Mel Carnahan greet a friendly "visitor" on the Mansion lawn. Camels, as well as reindeer, add to the festivities during the annual Candlelight Tours of the Mansion.

139

KEEPING CHRISTMAS

BY HENRY VAN DYKE

It is a good thing to observe Christmas Day,
The mere marking of times and seasons, when men agree to stop work
and make merry together, is a wise and wholesome custom.
It helps one to feel the supremacy of the common life over the individual life,
It reminds a man to set his own little watch, now and then,
by the great clock of humanity which runs of sun time.

But there is a better thing than the observance of Christmas Day,
and that is keeping Christmas.

Are you willing to forget what you have done for other people,
and to remember what other people have done for you;
to ignore what the world owes you, and to think what you owe the world;
to put your rights in the background, and your duties in the middle distance,
and your chances to do a little more than your duty in the foreground;
to see that your fellow men are just as real as you are,
and try to look behind their faces to their hearts hungry for joy;
to own that probably the only good reason for your existence
is not what you are going to get out of life, but what you are going to give to life;
to close your book of complaints against the management of the universe,
and look around you for a place where you can sow a few seeds of happiness—
are you willing to do these things even for a day?

THEN YOU CAN KEEP CHRISTMAS.

Are you willing to stoop down and consider the needs and the desires of
little children;
to remember the weakness and loneliness of people who are growing old;
to stop asking how much your friends love you,
and ask yourself whether you love them enough;
to bear in mind the things that other people have to bear in their hearts;
to try to understand what those who live in the same house with you really want,
without waiting for them to tell you;
to trim your lamp so that it will give more light and less smoke,
and to carry it in front so that your shadow will fall behind you;
to make a grave for your ugly thoughts and a garden for your kindly feelings,
with the gate open—
are you willing to do these things even for a day?

Then you can keep Christmas.

Are you willing to believe that love is the strongest thing in the world—
stronger than hate, stronger than evil, stronger than death—
and that the blessed life which began in Bethlehem nineteen hundred years ago
is the image and brightness of the Eternal Love?

Then you can keep Christmas.

And if you can keep it for a day, why not always?
But you can never keep it alone.

B. Gratz Brown
1871-1873

Silas Woodson
1873-1875

Charles Hardin
1875-1877

John Phelps
1877-1881

Thomas Crittenden
1881-1885

John Marmaduke
1885-1887

Albert Morehouse
1887-1889

David Francis
1889-1893

William Stone
1893-1897

Lon Stephens
1897-1901

Alexander Dockery
1901-1905

Joseph Folk
1905-1909

Missouri Governors   1871-1999

Herbert Hadley
1909-1913

Elliott Major
1913-1917

Frederick Gardner
1917-1921

Arthur Hyde
1921-1925

Samuel Baker
1925-1929

Henry Caulfield
1929-1933

Guy Park
1933-1937

Lloyd Stark
1937-1941

Forrest Donnell
1941-1945

Phil Donnelly
1945-1949; 1953-1957

Forrest Smith
1949-1953

James Blair
1957-1961

John Dalton
1961-1965

Warren Hearnes
1965-1973

Christopher Bond
1973-1977; 1981-1985

Joseph Teasdale
1977-1981

John Ashcroft
1985-1993

Mel Carnahan
1993-Present

The greatest glory of a building
is not in its stones or in its gold.

Its glory is in its age . . .

It is the lasting witness against men . . .
and the changing face of the earth . . . that connects
forgotten and following ages with each other.

~John Ruskin, 1849

ILLUSTRATION CREDITS

In crediting illustrations, the following abbreviations are used to indicate the image source, location on the page, alterations, photographer, and/or artist: *t*-top, *c*-center, *b*-bottom, *r*-right, *l*-left, *bck*-background, [d]-detail, [dc]-digitally corrected, [lr]-laterally reversed, [s]-screened, and [v]-vignette.

Sources:

AB - Alise O'Brien
CB - Corbis Bettmann
CCHS - Cole County Historical Society
CF - Carnahan Family
CPP - Crown Pantheon Publishers
DF - Donnell Family
DP - Dover Press
EL - Ellis Library—University of Missouri-Columbia
GC - Granger Collection
LBB - Little Bighorn Battlefield National Monument
MF - Massie Family
MFA - Museum of Fine Arts, Boston
MHP - Missouri Highway Patrol
MMPI - Missouri Mansion Preservation, Inc.
MSA - Missouri State Archives

MSC - Missouri State Capitol
RM - Robert Merck/Abbeville Press
SEK - Senator Edward Kennedy
SHS - The State Historical Society of Missouri
SLAM - The Saint Louis Art Museum
SM - Sating St. Marie
SO/AASLH - Sunny O'Neil/American Association for State and Local History
SWB - Southwestern Bell
TF - Teasdale Family
TL - Truman Library
UPI - United Press International/Corbis Bettmann
VDLM - *Victorian Decorating and Lifestyle*
WHMC - Western Historical Manuscripts Collection, University of Missouri-Columbia
WO - Whitey Owens

Dust jacket, endsheet, ii-iii, v, vi[d], vii, ix[d], x-xi [d]-MMPI; xii-CF; xiii-CCHS; xiv-MMPI; **1** SHS; **2** MMPI; **3** MMPI; **4** EL; **5** *t*-SM, *b*-DP; **6** SHS; **7** [v]-MMPI; **8** CPP; **9** *tl*-MMPI, *tr*-SHS, *b*[d]-DF; **11** *tl*[d]-TL/CB, *tr*-MSA, *b*-MF; **12** *tl*-CF, *tr*-CF, *cl*-MSA, *bl*-TF, *br*-CF; **13** *tl*-CCHS, *tr*-MMPI, *cr*-CCHS, *bl*-SHS, *br*-CF; **14** MMPI; **15** MMPI; **16** *tl*-CF, *tr*[d]-MMPI, *bl*[v]-MMPI, *br*[d]-MMPI; **17** MMPI; **18** MMPI; **19** DP; **20** *l*-RM, *tr*-DP; **21** [dc]-MMPI; **22** *tl*-MSA, *tr*[v]-MMPI, *bl*-MMPI; **23** *tl*[d]-MMPI, *tr-br*-MMPI; **24** MMPI; **25** SHS; **26** MMPI; **27** MMPI; **28** MMPI; **29** MMPI; **30** MMPI; **31** MMPI; **32-33** MMPI; **34** MMPI; **35** MMPI; **36** *tr*-MMPI, *bl*-RM; **37** DP; **38** MMPI; **39** *t-cl-cr-br*-MMPI, *bl*-SO/AASLH; **40-41** MMPI; **42** MMPI; **43** SHS; **44** MMPI; **45** MMPI; **46** MMPI; **47** *tr*-WHMC, *bl*-MSA; **48** MMPI; **49** (by column, *t* to *b*,[d]) *l*-LBB, SHS, CB, MMPI, CF; *c*-LBB, GC, TL, MMPI; *r*-UPI/CB, MSC, SEK, MMPI, CF; **50** MMPI; **51** [d]-MMPI; **52** MMPI; **53** VDLM; **55** MMPI; **57** MMPI; **58** MMPI; **60** MMPI; **62** [dc]-MMPI; **63** MSA; **65** MMPI; **66** MMPI; **68** [v]-MSA; **69** LBB; **71** MMPI; **72** MMPI; **73** MMPI; **75** MMPI; **77** [d]-WO; **79** MSA; **80** [d]-MMPI; **81** [d,s]-MMPI; **82** MMPI; **83** MMPI; **86** MMPI; **87** [v]-MMPI; **89** [v,dc]-MMPI; **91** MMPI; **92** MMPI; **93** [d,s]-MMPI; **95** MMPI; **99** SWB; **100** MMPI; **103** MMPI; **105** MFA; **106** MMPI; **107** MMPI; **108** MMPI; **111** MMPI; **112** MMPI; **118** EL; **122** EL; **123** MMPI; **124** SHS; **127** MMPI; **129** SHS; **130** CF; **135** MMPI; **139** MMPI; **142** (top row) [d]-MSC; (2nd row, *l* to *r*) [d]-MSC, [d]-SLAM, [d]-MSC, [d]-MSC, [d]-MSC, [d, lr]-MSC; (3rd row, *l* to *r*) [d]-MSC, [d]-MSC, [d]-MSC, [d]-MSC, [d, lr]-MSC; (4th row) [d]-MSC; (5th row, *l* to *r*) [d]-MSC, [d]-MSC, [d]-MSA, [d]-MHP, [d]-MSA, [d]-CF; **143** CF.

Photographers and Artists

Mary Pat Abele: 14, 16-*tr*, 26-*tl*, 38-*bl-cr*, 39-*cl-br*, 58, 93, 112, 139
Jamie G. Anderson: 12-*br*, 127-*sculpture* ©1994 Jamie G. Anderson. All rights reserved.
Roger Berg: 7, 13-*br*, 49-*r2*, 87, 142-*br*
Mary Cassatt: 105
Jim Dyke: 12-*tr*, 38-39-*t*
Hugo Harper and Neil Sauer: 22-*bl*, 34, 44-*t*, 49-*bkg*
Bob Hulsey: 16-*br*, 17-*l*, 83, 89, 135
Gerald Massie: 11-*b*, 13-*tl*, 52, 77

Alise O'Brien: Jacket front, jacket back-*bl-br* ii-iii, v, vi, ix, x-xi, xiv 3-*tr*, 13-*br bck*, 15-*t-br*, 17-*br*, 18, 21, 22-*tr*, 23, 24 ,26-*tr*, 27, 28, 30, 35, 36-*tr*, 40-41, 42, 44-*b*, 45, 48, 50, 51, 55, 57, 62 [d], 66, 71, 72, 73, 75, 80, 81, 82, 86, 91, 92, 95, 100, 103, 106, 107, 108, 111, 123, 127
Orval Reeves: 143
Gary Sutton: 62
Lisa Heffernan Weil: Jacket back-*t*, vii, 2-3, 15-*bl*, 16-*bl*, 17-*tr*, 26-*b*, 31, 32-33, 38-*br*, 39-*cr*, 49-*l4*
Ted Wofford: Endsheet, 29

A special thanks to these additional "elves" who have made Christmas at the Mansion so memorable: Facilities Management crew of Louie Wilbers, Martin Ward, Curtis Tellman, Bob Baldwin, Vern Wesley, Kendal Mertens, John Buechter, and Tim Lemport; Department of Natural Resources crew of Russell Rottmann, Bob Duncan, Terry Kuebler, and Debra Rademan; Conservation Department crew of Bruce Palmer, David Martz, Don Arnold, Ed Miller, Don Barns, Terry McDaniel, Jeff Petty, and Doug Starke; Bob Scott of Scott's Crane Service; Busch's crew of Holly Hyde, Cathy Schollmeyer, E. J. Rodgers, Robbie Fennewald, and Chad Munsey; Walsworth Publishing Company team of Don Walsworth, Steve Mull, Peter Fink, Scott Rule, Jeri Reese, Michelle North, and all the artists and technicians who helped along the way; Jim Maxey, Jimmy Jameson, Crystal Libbert, the Bob Bebe Family, and the numerous high school choral groups from across the state.

RECIPE INDEX

Appetizers and Buffet Dishes

Buffet Ham Loaves with Orange Sauce 112
Chicken Satay with Peanut Sauce 114
Crudités with Sesame Dip 117
Fresh Fruit with Yogurt Dip 115
Holiday Cranberry Punch 116
Hummus with Pistachio Nuts 109
Mini-Apple Muffins with
   Honey-Baked Ham 111, *111*
Pimiento Cheese Spread 110
Polenta Squares 115
Potato Boats 113
Snow Peas with Herb Cheese 113
South-of-the-Border Salsa 116
Spinach-Cheese Phyllo Triangles 110
Stuffed Mushrooms 111

Breads

Coconut Bread *100*, 105
Corn Muffins 84
Garlic Parmesan Bread 76
Mansion Dinner Rolls 60
Pumpkin Pecan Bread 93, *100*
Spoon Bread 124
Whole Wheat Dinner Loaves 69

Cookies and Tea Time Favorites

Black Walnut-Apple Bars 98
Cashew Cookies *100*, 104
Chocolate-Covered Cherry Cookies *100*, 103, *103*
Christmas Almond Bars 102
Cran-Apple Tartlets *100*, 107, *107*
Currant and Orange Scones 97
Featherlight Chocolate Chip Cookies 107
Lemon Tea Bread 101
Mini-Cheesecakes 99
Mint Brownies 106
Orange-Almond Biscotti 70
Orange-Nut Mocha Bars 117
Strawberry Bonnets 100, *100*
Tea Sandwiches 96, *100*
Vanilla Butter Buttons 91
Victorian Spiced Tea Punch 98

Desserts

Apricot Brandy Pound Cake 127
Cinnamon Ice Cream 79
Cranberry-Apple Frappé 121
Flaky Pie Crust 77
Fresh Fruit Compote 90, *91*
Orange Soufflé 85
Ozark Bread Pudding with Rum Sauce 126
Poached Pears with Raspberries 70, *71*
Pumpkin Cheesecake 61
Rum Raisin Apple Pie 78
Zabaglione Sauce 90

Entrees

Baja Chicken 134
Beef Brisket 137
Beef Medallion with Brandy Cream Sauce 56, *57*
Cashew Chicken 88
Chicken Chalupas 132
Chicken Marsala 131
Crab-Stuffed Prawns *57*, 58
Farfalle Carbonara 136
Maple Glazed Scallops 53
Nut-Encrusted Trout 131
Ozark Grilled Catfish 136
Pasta Primavera 139
Spaghetti Meat Sauce 135
Talapia with White Wine Sauce *66*, 67
Tarragon Lamb 132
Turkey Medallion Florentine 74, *75*

Salads and Dressings

Balsamic Vinaigrette 64
Basil Sauce 139
Basil Vinaigrette 54
Crunchy Romaine Toss 87
Curried Chicken Salad 83
Field Greens and Coconut Shrimp 73, *73*
Mixed Greens, Pears, and Gorgonzola 54, *55*
Mixed Greens with Hazelnut Encrusted Cheese 64
Mostaccioli Pasta Salad 109
Oriental Chicken Salad 133
Poppy Seed Dressing 128
Soy-Ginger Vinaigrette 133
Spinach Cashew Salad 128

Side Dishes

Asparagus with Orange Butter 57, *57*
Brussels Sprouts au Gratin 123, *123*
Cornbread Stuffing with Toasted Pecans 126
Corn Relish 125
Cranberry Sauce with Dried Cherries 125
Crusty Potato Galette *75*, 76
Eggplant Parmigiana 138
Garlic Potato Mounds *57*, 59
German Red Cabbage 119
Golden Risotto *66*, 68
Holiday Rice Casserole 129
Julienne Carrots and Zucchini 75, *75*

Mandarin Stir-Fried Rice 89
Roasted Mediterranean Vegetables 121
Old-Fashioned Applesauce 122
Orange-Glazed Sweet Potatoes 119
Squash Stir Fry 122
Sugar Snap Peas and Baby Carrots 65, *66*
Swiss Green Beans 128

Soups

Chicken Noodle Soup 134
Minestrone Soup with Pasta and Greens 138
Red Pepper and Potato Combo 81, *82*
Root Vegetable Soup *62*, 63